# BLACK DOLLS

## Proud, Bold & Beautiful

First edition/First printing

Copyright © 2004 Reverie Publishing Company. All rights reserved. No part of the contents of this book may be
reproduced without the written permission of the publisher.

To purchase additional copies of this book, please contact:
Reverie Publishing Company, 130 Wineow Street, Cumberland, MD 21502
888-721-4999

Library of Congress Catalog Card Number 2003097218
ISBN 1-932485-12-0

Project Editor: Joan Muyskens Pursley
Design and Production: Tammy S. Blank
Cover Design: John Vanden-Heuvel
On the cover: "Transcendence" by Marcella Welch
On the back cover, clockwise from top left: "Jazzy" by Sharon Tucker; "Henry" by Gloria Tepper;
"To Market" by Anne Myatt; "Madame Jubilee" by Tonia Mitchell Floyd

Printed and bound in Korea

# BLACK DOLLS
## Proud, Bold & Beautiful

Nayda Rondon

Introduction by Barbara A. Whiteman

Reverie

PUBLISHING COMPANY

# Contents

# Introduction

by Barbara A. Whiteman

*"This Great God,*
*Like a mammy bending over her baby,*
*Kneeled down in the dust*
*Toiling over a lump of clay*
*Till he shaped his own image."*

—*The Creation*, James Weldon Johnson

Most of us have held and loved dolls, and many of us have funny or sad stories to tell about them. These little images of ourselves are fascinating. They're poignant reminders of days past—of the innocence of youth, of childhood companions and, perhaps, of our daughters and sons and grandchildren. Quite often we are drawn to a doll because of a certain expression, such as a playful smile or twinkle in the eye. It is as if the doll speaks to us; we know, instantly, that it is meant to be ours. This is the magic of the doll and its mystical power, which keeps attracting us, whether we're children or adults.

Strangely, though dolls have played a role in most of our lives, whether as playmates, comforters or decorative objects in our homes, we often know little about their designers and makers, and about the thoughts and processes by which our prized dolls were created. How were the dolls' artists able to bring about this magic? Where did they get the *kuumba*—the creativity? Surely it is a gift from the ancestors. Long before a doll stood before you, the ancestors chose the doll's artist and endowed her or him with the magical power to create.

With each order to bring a doll to life, its artist must give up pieces of herself—not only her imagination, but her emotions and energies, until the image penetrates her soul and takes form. Then—and only then—does the doll present itself. Each doll creation is like a birth. From the first day of conception, a doll struggles for its own identity. It has its own personality and requires a certain style, fabric and color to authenticate its existence.

## The Doll Artist

The doll artist is a remarkable person, a person of extraordinary talents. These talents allow the dollmaker to capture an unbelievable life-like look in a miniature figure. It is beautifully surreal. The dollmaker's talent did not develop overnight; it has taken years of patience, lots of practice, and bundles of *imani*—faith. This talent is inspired by the doll artist's sensitivity to the beauty of a personality or to an expression of life. Each doll artist has an identifiable style that represents qualities inherent in her or his work. But in each and every doll, the artist also presents a "general principle of humanity," emphasizing the essence of the spirit within.

Beauty is in the "creative hands" of the beholder. These gracious hands belong to some of the world's most talented doll artists. What is in the hands of these artists may be cloth, porcelain or one of the various polymer clays—materials that serve as the dollmakers' palettes. The artists become research chemists who develop techniques in blending and firing clays in ovens or in kilns at incredibly high temperatures to create dolls with amazing skin tones. Some artists have the hands and patience of a skilled surgeon; they use their scalpels and other sculpting tools to manipulate and accentuate the clay faces of their dolls. Others use needles and thread to bring life to fabric. No matter what medium they use, these dollmakers have had to master a host of skills; not just the clay or needle sculpting, but also painting, wig making and hair design, pattern making and costume design. They must understand anatomy, color,

*Today's artists use a variety of materials for their dolls. "The Ballerina," above, is a 24-inch porcelain doll with a cloth body. It was created by Goldie Wilson. At left are dolls crafted from Super Sculpey, covered with knit. The 20-and-10-inch pair, by Anne Myatt, is titled "Chloe's Child."*

fashion. But perhaps even more important, these artists must have extraordinary imaginations. For the artist can only imagine what the doll will look like as it becomes more alive with each step of the creative process. Finally, texture and form design a beautiful idea, while balance and shape take the cloth or clay structure into the elegant human form we call a doll.

These doll artists expand the definition of a doll to be more than a three-dimensional representation of a human being, and more than just a toy for children; these contemporary doll artists are creating figurative sculpture. Sculpture is a three-dimensional art form, existing in space. The doll artists communicate ideas that are brought to life in the form of a doll. With a doll, our visual and tactile responses are so strong that we want to touch it, feel it to see if it is real. So often we say that the doll "looks like" someone we know, or that it is so haunting. Artistically, likeness, meaning physiognomy, is often regarded as the most significant single element of portraiture, particularly in Western art. The face or portrait, representational in form and naturalistic in style, is what we cherish most in dolls.

When we look into a doll's face, we establish the psychological connection with the doll.

The purpose of this book is to present to you the socio-historical context of dolls from the black diaspora and to celebrate doll artists who have released the beauty of dolls of color. Rather than challenging the traditional European perspective of beauty, the presentation of these dolls will allow readers to follow the history of black dolls to their present development and realities. This book presents the work of approximately fifty contemporary doll artists of various backgrounds and cultures. In profiling these artists, author Nayda Rondon explores their dynamic creation of dolls of color. Each doll presented is an outstanding example of artistic achievement. While the number of artists making black dolls is obviously not limited to those featured herein, this book provides a remarkable cross-section of currently available dolls of color. They range from handmade dolls filled with the charm of folk-art figures from the past to sleek and elegant fashion dolls from some of today's top designers.

7

## Early Clay Images

Historically, earth and water have always been associated with human life. Since Africa is considered the cradle of mankind, we can imagine that some million years ago early man manipulated river mud into clay to form images of himself and his gods and goddesses. He discovered that the clay was malleable, and he could use it to make various shapes and images. He also discovered that when left to bake in the sun, the clay hardened into statuettes or dolls that retained their shapes.

Images of clay dolls are universal, and shared by all cultures separated and distinguished by time and geography. It is in fired clay that we find many of the earliest forms of sculpture.

For thousands of years the ancient Egyptians and Nubians made small statues of human beings to put in royal tombs along with the king's treasures. It was believed that these "beings" would assist the king in his new life in the afterworld. Many of these small-size clay images, called Ushabtis, have been recovered from Egyptian graves—some dating from as far back as 1500 B.C.E.

The earliest images of West Africans were found in Nigeria. They were made by the Nok culture between 500 B.C.E. and circa 200 C.E. The people of Nok were highly skilled in the art of making sculptures of life-size human figures—figures that must have been four or more feet in height. The sculptors were able to fire them successfully, an extremely difficult task in uncontrolled open flames. The heads of these Nok sculptures are noted for being highly conceptualized representations, exhibiting great vitality and vivid expressions.

Later Nigerian sculpture is equally notable. The art of the Yoruba people at Ife (Nigeria, 600 to 900 C.E.), who believed that the deity Obatala created humanity from clay, is extraordinary in representing human beings with a realism that makes them almost portrait-like in appearance. They appear to depict the actual physical characteristics of the individual rather than offering generalized images.

Other groups in Africa, as well as the early peoples of Asia and the Americas, also created clay figures representing the human form. Some of these were associated with burial customs, some were created for religious rites and some were decorative. There is little doubt that some figures also were made by children at play.

Of course, representations of the human form also played a role in European culture through the centuries. Early classic Greek sculptors idealized the human body, believing that it was the most beautiful gift they could offer the gods. The sculptors of ancient Rome became more interested in recording the faces of actual human beings than in creating idealized portraits.

*This rare, unmarked Chase doll has an oil-painted stockinette head and a jointed cloth body with sateen covering. Its caracul wig is original. The 27-inch doll sold for $5,700 at McMasters Harris's November 9, 2002, auction. (Photo: McMasters Harris Auction Company)*

*This very rare "Kaiser Baby" has a bisque head and a composition body. The 11-inch doll sold for $700 at a McMasters Harris 2002 auction. The back of its head is marked "23//K★R//100." (Photo: McMasters Harris Auction Company)*

## Materials

Dolls can be produced in any material that can be worked into a human form. In addition to clay, early dolls were made out of twigs, clothespins, carved and turned wood. Dolls have also been made from all sorts of fabric and leather. Then there are wax dolls, china dolls, tin dolls, papier-mâché dolls and dolls made of china, bisque and porcelain. (Ever popular, porcelain dolls are made from very fine white kaolin clays and are fired in kilns at temperatures close to 3000 degrees Fahrenheit.) In the twentieth century, doll artists made use of an increasing number of new materials, including rubber, vinyl, plastic and various polymer clays.

Today's doll artists enjoy experimenting with all types of fabric and textiles for the doll bodies as well as for costuming. In expressing their ideas, doll artists understand the nature of fabrics and have the opportunity to choose from a wide variety, from natural fibers such as cottons, to animal fibers such as silks, or synthetics, such as nylon, to get the desired effect. These fabrics may be oil painted, molded or needle-sculpted; in the hands of an artist, they are as flexible as the clays.

Doll artists know that many collectors admire a doll for the emotions it evokes, rather than because of the materials from which it is made. So, doll artists continue to experiment with new materials and to develop new techniques. The newest materials used in making dolls are the synthetic resins, polymer clays as well as paperclays. Polymer clays are soft thermosetting plastics that were developed in a chemist's laboratory. Unlike natural clay from the earth, polymer clays can be baked in a home oven. At temperatures from 212 to 275 Fahrenheit, the particles in these clays undergo chemical changes, which cause them to fuse and retain their solid shape. One-of-a-kind doll artists especially appreciate the polymer clays because dolls made from them do not require molds or kiln firing, as do porcelain dolls.

*By Gebruder Kuhnlenz, this 7½-inch mammy and baby brought $600 at a McMasters Harris 2002 sale. Marked "34.17" on the back of its bisque sockethead, the black doll wears the original dress and carries an unjointed bisque baby. (Photo: McMasters Harris Auction Company)*

These new materials, along with sculpting techniques, help the doll artist to capture the spirit of the self-image. Can it be that these dolls engage us to recognize ourselves, what we were or want to be? We are intrigued by the face, ever changing and so different. The face can be complicated and exacting. In wordless communication, the face captures the moment, revealing expressions and attitudes.

## Dolls of Color in Europe

In reviewing the achievements of the Golden Age of doll artistry in Europe (1875-1920) author Stuart Holbrook states in his book, *The Doll as Art* (Theriault's Gold Horse Publishing, 1990), "The beauty and quality of a doll was determined by the face, form, and fashion." Dolls made in France and Germany were the best that Europe offered. Most dolls were mass manufactured and the emphasis was on the doll and not the individual artist. Only a few doll manufacturers employed noted sculptors, such as Albert Marque, to create unique doll faces.

The French doll manufacturers such as Jumeau and Bru Jne. & Cie. were reputed to have the prettiest faces, notably, those with the enormous blown-glass paperweight eyes. These "pretty" dolls represented what the dollmakers of the past believed was the ultimate in feminine beauty.

Firms in both France and Germany manufactured what were called "exotic dolls"—dolls that represented non-European people. These dolls were carefully painted in a variety of hues and complexions. Black dolls were fanatically dressed in tribal or ethnic clothing. These exotic dolls were successful due to the curiosity about and interest in peoples of other cultures.

Were dolls of color considered beautiful? Yes, by all standards. We know that beautiful is defined as that which gives us sensuous, emotional or aesthetic pleasure. Beauty exists in all colors and cultures. Technically, the flesh color of bisque is controlled by the artistry and the color sense of the manufacturer, since it is an artificial color applied to the clay between kiln firings. This color, really a glaze, sinks into the porous surface of the clay and is fused, making it permanent. In fired-in-bisque dolls, the head and other doll parts are painted black after the initial firing of the bisque and then re-fired at a lower temperature to set the color.

The German doll manufacturers competitively beat the French in doll production. They also led the way in reforming and designing dolls to produce what were called "character" dolls, designs that represented realism through more human-looking faces. (Many doll heads from German manufacturers were exported to France, where they were attached to bodies.) Although not designated at the time, the European artists who

*Made in Germany by Simon & Halbig, this brown-skinned doll has a bisque sockethead—featuring an open mouth with four teeth—and a jointed wood and composition body. The 20½-inch doll brought $600 at McMasters Harris's April 5, 2003 sale. (Photo: McMasters Harris Auction Company)*

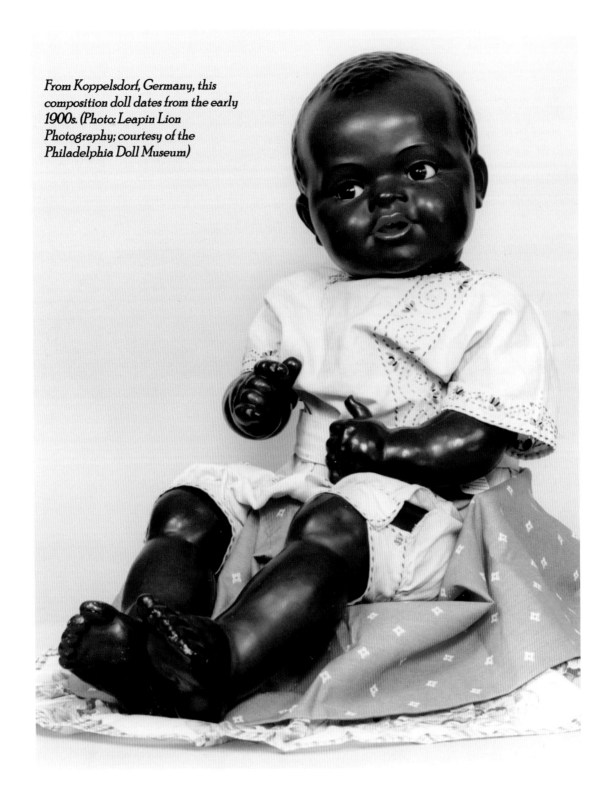

were responsible for those new doll face designs were the precursors of today's doll artists. Graduating from the old "dolly blank stares with closed mouths," the new facial features of the character dolls displayed mischievous smiles, open or watermelon mouths, flirting, side-glancing eyes, molded teeth, tongues, even dimples. Besides crying, the new character dolls could whistle, laugh, frown or appear to be screaming, reflecting a realm of human emotions.

## Early Black Dolls in America

At the beginning of the nineteenth century, few American children played with dolls imported from Europe. Most of the dolls found in this country were handmade by the children's parents, relatives or local artisans. These dolls were made from various materials, including wood, corncobs, nuts, and even tobacco leaves. Also common were "rag" or cloth dolls made from discarded clothing. Black cloth dolls were made by both black and white per-

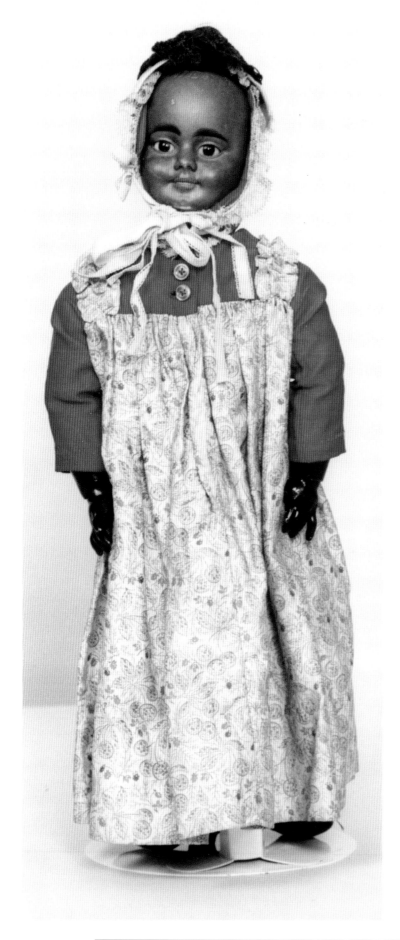

*The black and brown faces of this multi-faced porcelain doll are seen here. From Belton, Germany, it dates from the early 1900s. (Photo: Leapin Lion Photography; courtesy of the Philadelphia Doll Museum)*

sons whose children loved and played with them.

A very popular black doll made during the early 1900s was the handmade cloth "mammy" doll, which represented generations of enslaved black women. This black-face doll was easily recognized by her white head wrap and white apron. Most of the time she was robust in size, carrying a white baby, and she always wore a smile. It was this smile that later became caricaturized into a large, unappealing grin.

Many black dolls created by white Americans were not made in the image of black children or adults, but rather were caricatures designed to support views of racial superiority. These black dolls were crudely made with demeaning and exaggerated facial features. Black children would not play with such derogatory dolls, nor would black parents purchase them.

The negative images projected by the caricature dolls supported a theory of racial inferiority and instilled

low esteem in black children. In 1908, ministers from the National Baptist Convention asked the doll and toy manufacturers to make more favorable colored dolls for colored children. By 1920, so-called "colored" dolls began being manufactured along with white dolls. These colored dolls had no ethnic features; they were simply painted version of white composition dolls. For decades, doll manufacturers continued to darken the skin tones of play dolls, in an effort to market them to African Americans. Indeed, as late as 1981 Ideal Toy Corporation introduced a black Patti Playpal that was simply a dark version of its Caucasian model.

There were a few doll artists in the early decades of the twentieth century who created positive black images in dolls along with their white doll creations. Emma Adams (born in 1890) of Oswego, New York; Julia Jones Beecher (1893) of Elmira, New York; and Martha Jenks Chase (1851) of Pawtucket, Rhode Island, are fine examples of such doll artists. Another exceptional doll artist of that period was Rosa Wilder Blackman of Homer, Louisiana; in the 1920s, she created black clay dolls depicting her hometown black neighbors. Each doll's character was dignified, and each one was dressed in ordinary, everyday outfits.

Where are the black dolls of the 1920s and 1930s? Are these black dolls rare? We know that black dolls are not rare, but they are difficult to find today because most of the early positive images of black children have been literally loved to pieces. We can tell that some dolls have a special "aura" about them that seems to proclaim the doll was important to someone and has been especially loved.

## The Doll "Test"
In the 1940s, in a classic study designed to document the impact of negative racial images on children, two black social scientists, Dr. Kenneth Clark and his wife, Dr. Mamie P. Clark, used two brown and two white dolls to study the effects of segregated schools on black children by measuring the attitudes of black children toward race. Black children chose the white dolls as the "best," the "nicest" and the "prettiest." The result of the test demonstrated to the Clarks how young black children learned prevailing social ideas about racial differences

*Left: This unmarked primitive cloth doll is 19 inches high. It has embroidered features and is jointed at the shoulders, hips and knees. Very well made and dressed, it brought $500 at a McMasters Harris 2003 sale. Right: these primitive cloth dolls are also unmarked. The 25-inch black doll has exaggerated facial features, including an oversize mouth filled with tiny teeth. It sold for $1,100 at a 2003 McMasters Harris sale. The 24-inch oil-painted doll sold for $2,500 at the same sale. (Photos: McMasters Harris Auction Company)*

*Above: These floppy cloth dolls date from the 1930s; they were made in America by an unknown craftsperson. Left: Topsy-turvy cloth dolls like this one, featuring one black face and one white one, were not uncommon at the end of the nineteenth and beginning of the twentieth centuries. (Photos: Leapin Lion Photography; courtesy of the Philadelphia Doll Museum)*

early in their lives, and "that black children who received segregated, inferior education came to feel inferior themselves."

As a result of the low number of positive black dolls on the American market, and the increase in black consciousness motivated through the Civil Rights Movement, there was an increase in the number of black-owned companies making black dolls. Some of the black manufacturers were: The National Negro Doll Company (founded in 1910), Beatrice W. Brewington— The First Negro Toy Company (1965), Tan Line (1968), Shindana Toy Company (1968), Keisha Doll Company (1981), Lomel Enterprises (1985), Golden Ribbon Playthings (1985) and Olmec (1985). These manufacturers created ethnically correct dolls and action figures that reinforced positive self-images and helped counteract the effects of negative racial images.

Depicting Little Black Sambo, this American-made cloth doll is 22 inches high. Stamped on its lower back, jacket and shoes are: "WPA//Handicraft//Project #8601//Milwaukee//Wisconsin//Sponsored by//Milwaukee//County and//Milwaukee//State Teachers//College" and "Designed by//Helen Clark." The doll, which sold for $1,850 at McMasters Harris's November 9, 2002, American Heritage auction, has a painted stockinette head with curly black cotton-string hair and a brown cloth body. (Photo: McMasters Harris Auction Company)

*I. Roberta Bell created these dolls, which she issued under the name Bertabel's Dolls. They depict, from left: Harriet Tubman, Reverend Richard Allen, Sojourner Truth, Dr. George Washington Carver and Frederick Douglas. (Photo: Leapin Lion Photography; courtesy of the Philadelphia Doll Museum)*

## Black Doll Artists in America

When considering early black doll artists in America, two names stand out: Leo Moss and I. Roberta Bell.

Leo Moss was a self-taught doll artist from Macon, Georgia. He began making dolls in the 1890s and continued to create them into the early 1930s. Family members were the main subjects of his work. His artistic talent was recognized in his community, and he received many commissions to create portrait dolls of children. He made both black and white dolls.

One of his surviving dolls, "BoBo," has a mischievous look on his face and his tongue is sticking out. A few of his dolls smile; others appear pensive or serene. Most of his dolls, however, have very sad faces and tears flowing down their checks. According to doll historian and author Myla Perkins (*Black Dolls 1820-1991*, Collector Books, 1993), Moss began incorporating tears on his dolls after a number of toddlers who were posing for portrait dolls became impatient and began to cry.

All Moss dolls were individually made, and no two dolls are alike. They have papier-mâché heads with molded hair in a variety of styles, including cornrows and braided coils. Moss used a spray gun for the initial painting of his dolls; boot dye and stove blacking formed the base color for them. The arms and legs were made of old composition. Glass eyes were always brown and were inset into the dolls' molded heads. He simply signed his dolls "L.M."

Leo Moss was certainly not the only black artist or handcrafter to make black dolls at the turn of the twentieth century, but perhaps because of the ingenious way he was able to portray the emotions of his subjects, a number of his dolls have survived. As portraits of actual children, they may have been cherished by adults, rather than given to youngsters for strenuous play.

Born in 1904, I. Roberta Bell was part of a very religious and artistic family. She herself told me the story of how her minister father, Robert, an artist and sculptor, made black dolls for her by removing the heads and limbs from white dolls. Much to her dismay, her father taught her brother to draw and paint but neglected to teach her.

Although she loved dolls and was determined to make them, her education came first. She received master's degrees in sociology and education. After these studies, she took all courses necessary to become proficient in dollmaking: ceramic classes, china painting and mold-making. Unhappy with the paint colors available to her, she mixed her own, experimenting with various china paints to get appropriate skin coloring for her dolls.

Bell was a natural sculptor. Art and history were the themes for her line of portrait dolls, titled Famous Black American Dolls. The first doll in this line depicted Dr. George Washington Carver, a scientist whom she had met as a child. As a result of her "special excellence" in creating the Carver doll, Bell was elected to membership in the prestigious National Institute of American Doll Artists (NIADA) in 1970. She died in 1992.

## Historical Ethnic Dolls in America

In addition to the work of individual artists and small, black-owned doll companies, major American doll and toy makers have issued black dolls over the years. Among the first were of these dolls were "Amosandra," "Bonnie Lou," "Patty Jo" and "Saralee."

On Valentine's Day, 1949, a "colored" rubber doll named "Amosandra" appeared in stores. She was a promotional doll for *Amos and Andy*, the popular CBS radio program, and was designed to represent the baby daughter of the show's Amos and Ruby characters. "Amosandra" was designed by Ruth E. Newton as a nursing baby. The doll was packaged with numerous play items, but most importantly, she was the first doll to come with a birth certificate.

"Bonnie Lou" and "Patti Jo" are products of the Terri Lee Doll Company, which was founded by Violet Gradwohl in 1946. "Bonnie Lou" was the California-based company's first black doll. One assumes that it was successful, as in 1947 the company commissioned Zelda "Jackie" Ormes, a black woman, to produce another black doll; this one would be called "Patti Jo." Ormes was an artist and the first nationally syndicated female cartoonist. Characters "Patti Jo," big sister "Ginger" and "Torchy Brown," a paper doll, were featured in the *Pittsburgh Courier*, a national Negro newspaper.

Ormes designed her own doll and used the brown toned "Bonnie Lou" to create, in three-dimensional form, her cartoon protegé, "Patti Jo." Ormes taught company artists the proper way to paint the new "Patti Jo" dolls. Distinguished from the "Bonnie Lou" doll, the "Patti Jo" doll has two ponytails, a larger mouth, and dramatic eyebrows and eyelashes. The doll was advertised as the "NICEST BROWN DOLL" you ever saw. In a little story by Ormes that was inserted in each doll package, she expresses her hopes that the doll "may bring a bit more happiness to kids of all races." In 1951 the company no longer produced "Patti Jo"; however, it did issue a black Terri Lee under the name of the old "Bonnie Lou" doll.

*The little doll in the red-checked dress and bonnet is "Amosandra," a 1930s rubber baby doll that promoted the popular Amos and Andy radio program. With her is "Saralee" (sporting a yellow-and-white dress with matching bonnet) and two composition dolls. (Photo: Leapin Lion Photography; courtesy of the Philadelphia Doll Museum)*

*Left: "Bonnie Lou" and "Benji" were created by the Terri Lee Sales Corporation. "Bonnie Lou" wears a red-dotted Swiss Heart Fund dress topped by a white pinafore. "Benji" is dressed in a short red overall and a long-sleeved white shirt. (Photo: Leapin Lion Photography; courtesy of the Philadelphia Doll Museum)*

Sara Lee Creech, of Belles Glade, Florida, is the creator of "Saralee," which was billed as a "Negro Doll." Creech, a white social worker, believed that Negro (the word she used at that time for African Americans) children should have a doll of their own—one that looked like them. To make sure that the doll would be anthropologically correct, Creech photographed and measured the heads of three-to-eight-year-old African-American children; from these details, she developed a composite picture for the doll. Using Creech's detailed head measurements, sculptress Sheila Burlingame was able to create four model heads with accurate features.

In 1953, Ideal Doll Company manufactured the "Saralee" doll. A jury of prominent and distinguished persons, including Eleanor Roosevelt, Dr. Ralph Bunche, and NAACP president Walter White, were selected to determine the doll's skin color. This beautiful toddler doll's head and limbs are made of a soft vinyl material; its body is cloth. Included on the label on its box is: "Saralee Negro Doll//More Than Just a Doll...An Ambassador of Good Will."

Saralee was not the only black doll to be issued by Ideal. The New York company, founded in 1904 by Morris Mitchtom, also produced black versions of its popular Crissy, Baby Crissy and Patti Playpal. These dolls, however, appear to be dark-skinned versions of their white counterparts.

Since the 1950s, a number of other American companies have created black dolls, including Alexander Doll Company, Mattel, The Ashton-Drake Galleries, Tonner Doll Company, Daddy's Long Legs/KVK and Seymour Mann. Some of these dolls are designed specifically for play, but others hold more appeal for adult doll collectors. What's significant is that, finally, doll and toy companies are creating dolls that truly reflect the bone structure and features of the various black cultures.

## In Conclusion

The interest in artist dolls is explosive! As early as the 1950s, artists seem to have said, "I can make a better doll" than those they saw on the commercial market. The emphasis was on creativity and individual doll artistry, on honest and realistic portrayals of people of all races.

Through trial and error, these doll artists released dormant and latent talents. Working in home kitchens and studios, artists began to demonstrate their plans to create dolls that would meet our emotional needs and our fantasies. Motivated by deep personal feelings and imagery, doll artists touch our emotions each time we look at one of their creations. We became impressed and involved by the expressive form of doll art.

Today's doll artists are creating realistic images that people of other cultures can relate to globally. They may

*"Patti Jo Calypso"* is also from Terri Lee Sales Corporation. The 16-inch hard-plastic doll is in her original dress and white leatherette shoes. The fruit, which hangs from her original black wig and wrist, is made of papier-mâché. (Photo: McMasters Harris Auction Company)

include the classic Greek and Western ideas of beauty, but they also go beyond them to discover the aesthetic of other cultures. The concern of people of color is whether doll artists will make dolls of color that evoke emotions of the black experience. To create and promote dolls of the African diaspora, doll artists have the responsibility of knowing and caring about all peoples of color. According to Keith Morrison, "Color is becoming a descriptive term, an adjective to describe the differences in hue, rather than a noun to describe a race. As color distinctions proliferate, white may become not a race apart, but another color among many."

As doll lovers and art lovers, we must agree with Eleanor Roosevelt when she said, "We need to develop an audience for our artists of every kind...that the power to appreciate is often just as important as the power to actually create." What we appreciate about our doll artists is the need to express our emotions and their capability to interpret life in our pluralistic society and diversified world.

A combination of paperclay and fabric, Marcella Welch's "Transcendence" is a 28-inch seated doll.

# The Dolls and Their Makers

# AUDREY BELL & GEORGETTE TAYLOR

*"Bravo to this dynamic duo who had the wonderful foresight to create lovable, buxom beauties with femininity personified. These glamorous dolls can definitely meet any challenge as they are struttin' and groovin' with attitude and flair."—BAW*

Big and beautiful themselves, Audrey Bell and Georgette Taylor didn't have to look far for inspiration for their dolls, which they conceptualize and produce under the company name of Big Beautiful Dolls.

They've only been making dolls since 1999 and selling them since 2002, but they've already created quite a buzz with their fashion divas, which are big on attitude and presence. The motto of the dolls—and their creators—is: "Don't let what you weigh stand in your way of achieving any and all your dreams."

"We know that our dolls are different," states Bell, "but we did not know that we would get such a great reception from doll collectors. They've all been so wonderful, accepting us as the new kids on the block. We are just now entering mainstream, and we are loving every minute of it."

The dolls have been featured on numerous local and national television and radio programs, as well as in women's and doll magazines. "Dasia," the duo's African-American doll, was nominated for a prestigious *DOLLS* Award of Excellence in 2002. Although "Dasia" didn't win, the women of Big Beautiful Dolls weren't fazed. "Losing is always a downer, but there is always next year," says the ever-confident and upbeat Bell.

Taylor shares Bell's drive and enthusiasm for a business that's turned into a calling. After meeting at a seminar, the two statuesque beauties quickly found they had much in common and became friends. Bell, realizing there were no big-sized dolls on the market, suggested to Taylor, a doll collector, that they come out with one themselves. Soon the enterprising pair was taking it from idea to action. They found a designer and manufacturer, and voila—three full-figured beauties in vinyl.

Designed by Bell and Taylor in Bell's likeness, the dolls, which are sculpted by Donna Vernal, include "Dasia," an African American described as the publisher of a lifestyle magazine; "Dena," a Latina, who is the magazine's senior photographer; and "Dawn," a Caucasian, who is the fashion editor. Each is limited to 2,500 pieces. Their next group of dolls will be issued in smaller editions of 250 and 150 pieces. Ranging from twelve to twenty inches high, the dolls are priced from $59 to about $250.

"Although Barbie is considered beautiful, she does not represent the sixty-two-percent of us who are a size

14 and up," Bell states. "I have been full-figured all of my life. I know the issues that women deal with when they are overweight. I wanted to create a company dedicated to helping women feel good about who they are."

"We're using the dolls not only as a product, but as a service, too," adds Taylor. "I'm attracted to portraying dolls of black characters; they are very needed to show the beauty and diversity of our culture. Just as we are as a people, African-American dolls can be so diverse in character. We want to portray that through our dolls."

Bell and Taylor are carrying the banner not only for full-figured women and African Americans but for other minorities as well. At least seventy-five percent of their work is devoted to ethnic subjects. "We thought it was not only important to show another size, but to be realistic in showing other nationalities in that size, too," Taylor explains.

Confident and talented, these women have a message that is loud and clear. "Our company and dolls are set apart. We created history with the Big Beautiful Doll Collection, the first full-figured fashion dolls," Taylor says with justifiable pride. "There are and will be other dolls to follow, but we made it there first. In the process we have learned how important it is to keep going and doing what you believe in. We have learned a lot on our road, and we love sharing that information with others."

*"Dasia,"*
*12 inches, vinyl*

# FLOYD BELL

*"A gifted and meticulous artist, Floyd follows the lead of his ancient craftsmen by infusing the spirit of 'humanness' in his wood images. Bell's dolls are natural in their posing and intrinsically creative." —BAW*

**I**t seems that I am only happy when I am meeting new challenges and creating," says Floyd Bell. "I have always loved to show my work—be it building a house, upholstering fine furniture, writing a song or playing the guitar. Creating something new for the world to enjoy is what I am about."

This Renaissance man, whose "day job" is teaching industrial arts to high school students, counts dollmaking among his chief talents. Bell made his first doll—a peg-jointed figure he'd seen in a how-to magazine—as a classroom project to motivate his students, many of them inner city youths, to use their imaginations and skills.

Before long, Bell's "little project" became the class pet, stimulating his students to create their own dolls and Bell to delve further into dollmaking. Upon the suggestion of his wife, Sandra, a doll collector, he signed up for a class in porcelain face painting. When his teacher mentioned that the original bodies for these types of dolls were carved from wood, Bell asked if he could carve his own doll's body. "She said it would be difficult and doubted that I could do it," recalls Bell, who remained determined to try. "I carried my doll head around to doll shops and asked if I could see a French body so I could carve a body for my porcelain head. I met Mary Mason, who owned a doll shop and hospital. Mary saw that I was on the road to becoming a doll artist. She brought out a French body and told me to keep it as long as I wanted. The body was in fifteen pieces. It was quite a challenge, but I was up to it. My first porcelain doll was beautiful."

Four months later, Bell was working on his "Black Rascals," original black dolls carved from walnut wood and with German blown-glass eyes. These dolls were the forerunners of Bell's popular Country Kids series.

Becoming increasingly immersed in the world of dolls, he started to realize that there weren't many black dolls, and those that were available were far from anything he—by now an unabashed collector himself—might want, with their "grotesque black features, such as big lips and bulging eyes." When he compared these black dolls with the parade of white dolls, Bell thought, "perhaps there is a market for beautiful black dolls and meaningful historical black figures."

*"African Lady," 26 inches, wood*

This idea gave birth to Belle Dolls in 1980, and soon Bell—aided by seamstress Doris Parker, who helped design many of the historical costumes—was producing his American Heritage Doll series, which has come to consist of more than forty different dolls.

"Creating black dolls of great Americans who contributed to our rich culture gives black people a sense of pride in their race," Bell asserts. "Making beautiful black dolls gives children and adults an opportunity to see black people in a positive light."

Bell's own brilliance has earned him numerous awards and distinctions. In addition to private collections, places such as the Louvre Museum in Paris, France, the Wanke Doll Museum in Germany, and Le Musée de Poupees collection in Morbihan, France, showcase his dolls. In 1991, he was inducted into the prestigious National Institute of American Doll Artists (NIADA). His dolls have been featured in movies and CNN documentaries, graced the White House Christmas tree, and been used in fundraising efforts for the Floyd Bell Scholarship Foundation, a non-profit organization Bell and his family operated for several years to raise college funds for underprivileged youths.

Yet, despite all the public acclaim and rewards, Bell's family remains his greatest source of inspiration, satisfaction and support. "My mom, Modie Bell, was my favorite critic. She always made me feel like I was doing a great thing when I created something. When I had my final visits with her in the hospital, I can still hear her say, 'you just keep on making them dolls. Child, that's something that you thought up all on your own.'"

He may have thought of it all by himself, but by now it's become a true family affair. Bell, whose doll tastes run to antiques, and period and character pieces, was enticed by his then seven-year-old granddaughter, Toni, to make her a "pretty doll like Barbie." The result: a lithe and lovely black doll made entirely of jelutong wood. This doll eventually led Bell to develop and sell a line of cast-resin dolls, as well as a line of do-it-yourself Toni's Fashion Dolls kits. Although he's worked in several mediums, wood remains his favorite. His work ranges in price from $150 for the resin Country Kids to $10,000 for one-of-a-kind pieces like "African Lady," a proud woman of walnut.

Bell, who currently makes about ten dolls a year, clearly crafts each piece with love and care. "I'm not interested in making money; I want my dolls to bring joy and to have meaning. I work with the features until I can see and feel a part of myself in my work. Museum curators have told me that my dolls seem to have a soul of their own.

*Opposite page: "Jane Pitman," 18 inches, wood (Photo: W. Donald Smith); Right: "Ella Fitzgerald," 22 inches, wood*

"My dolls tell a story of a great people in Diaspora from the Motherland, Africa," Bell continues. "I tell of a people torn from their homeland and enslaved in foreign lands. In the faces of my dolls, I try to capture the pain and suffering, the dignity and resolve of a people who endured."

Ever the history lover, Bell continues to expand upon the characters in his American Heritage series. He is also exploring African Heritage, most notably with his Nomadic Family pieces. "I guess you could say I'm working my way back. First I looked at our American roots and now I'm reaching back to our African connections."

Moms—and granddaughters—really do know best, and luckily for collectors and admirers everywhere, Bell has heeded the loving counsel of his womenfolk. Linking the present with the past, he continues to create a legacy of pride, achievement and beauty as strong and enduring as the wood wonders his hands bring to life.

# SANDRA MILLER BLAKE

*"Collectors love Sandra's fascinating talent for creating realistic dolls with genuine warmth and emotion. Embodied with vitality, these beautiful dolls, usually made of polymer clays, emulate feelings of peace and pride, insuring us that there is hope for the world."—BAW*

Born on July 1, 1947, in Columbia, South Carolina, Sandra Miller Blake has been immersed in all things "dollightful" since she won the Blue Ribbon for her collection of handmade clothing at the South Carolina State Fair when she was twelve years old. Her passion for fabric design led her to Howard University where, in 1973, she earned a Bachelor of Sciences degree in clothing and textiles. While at Howard, she says, she learned to fully value the history and beauty of her black heritage. After becoming a mother, she sought to pass along this sense of pride to her two children, and she looked for but found few acceptable dolls to serve as positive depictions of black children. Her enterprising solution—to fashion her own.

"The first doll was made from a bought pattern," says Blake. "It lit a flame. I started to research dolls, making and collecting them, and found that there wasn't much out there. Black dolls were usually just white dolls

"*Ngoma,*"
*12 inches, wax over polymer clay*

painted black. In the midst of the era of 'Black Pride' I felt a strong urge to make dolls for my daughter, and for other children and their mothers, that reflected our beauty and heritage."

In 1978, Blake—aided by her husband, James Blake—founded Sanjean Originals. The company premiered with a line of her original cloth dolls, the "Dollightful Family," which consisted of a father, a mother, a boy and a girl, as well as a baby. These were sold by mail as patterns. Gradually Blake added various new designs, including "Jingles" and "Belle," a family of black elves, and a full-sized, well-proportioned doll depicting a two-year-old and titled "Learning Lizzie."

The Sanjean line continued to grow in direct proportion to Blake's interest in and exploration of different media options and subject matter. The artist started working in porcelain clay in the early 1980s, and her attention to facial and body modeling, mold production and costuming detail allowed her to produce many noteworthy pieces. Her cast of characters encompassed historical figures, such as Martin Luther King, Jr. and Joe Louis, and entertainers like Sammy Davis, Jr., Bill Cosby and Oprah Winfrey. Yet many collectors will argue that her greatest pieces are those that spring from Blake's imagination—charming and appealing personalities such as a little African drummer boy, a black newborn in her christening gown and a glowing black bride blissfully heading toward the altar and her beloved. The one underlying central theme present in all her work—past and present—is a positive depiction of family, friends and black role models.

"I love the process of creating dolls. Designing, sculpting and working in the different media just adds to the excitement," says the artist, who has worked in cloth, porcelain, resin and polymer clay. She designs about six dolls a year; each is an original sculpture, hand-painted, hand-wigged and costumed in handmade original designs.

Blake creates both one-of-a-kind and limited-edition pieces. "I make limited editions of up to 250 pieces, though smaller editions of twenty-five to fifty are more comfortable to create," she notes. Her one-of-a-kind pieces are priced at $1,200 and up, while her limited editions start at $200; the dolls range in size from thirteen to eighteen inches.

Often commissioned by individuals, organizations and businesses to create original porcelain dolls, Blake was selected, in 1994, to design and make the limited-edition doll that would represent that year's National Black Arts Festival. Titled "Ascension," it features a beautiful black woman dancing and reaching for the heavens and was well received, leading to many other commissions. Blake proudly recounts that one of her most rewarding and challenging assignments was the design and creation of a doll, patented by Dr. Smith-Whitley of the Children's Hospital of Philadelphia, to allow physicians to teach parents and patients about the effects of sickle-cell anemia on the body.

Blake, who continues to create new doll designs from her home studio in Blythewood, South Carolina, also works as a designer and patternmaker for a costume production company in her town. Most recently, she has added teaching others to make cloth dolls to her professional resumé.

Although she emphasizes that she doesn't restrict her art to dolls of any one type or race ("Making dolls has awakened my senses to the beauty in the diversity of people," she remarks), she does admit that black dolls hold a pivotal place in her work. "Very few people are doing it," she notes. "I want to leave a legacy." Intent on

*Above left: "Phillea," 23 inches, resin;*
*Top right: "Ahmad," 10 inches, porcelain;*
*Above: "Teddi Loves Tweed," 18 inches, seated, paper*
*clay over cloth*

leaving her mark, she creates distinctive pieces that she terms "realistic" in style; Blake "wants the viewer to feel that they are in the presence of friends and family" when they look at the dolls she fashions. In order to achieve the highest degree of verisimilitude, she does as much research and gathers as many pictures of each subject as she can in order to get to know her characters. Her ultimate goal is to create pieces that inspire pride, wonder and recognition.

# MARTHA BOERS & MARIANNE REITSMA

*"Martha and Marianne bring a wealth of artistic versatility to all of their creations. Let's hope that they continue to enrich our lives through dolls of all colors." —BAW*

Sisters Martha Boers and Marianne Reitsma never quite outgrew the practice of playing dolls together. From the start it was the perfect combination. Martha, eight years the senior, loved to make things, and Marianne, imaginative and lively, liked nothing better than to play.

Martha learned to knit at the tender age of three and by six was a whiz with a sewing needle; she would sew doll costumes and make elaborate props for Marianne and her friends to play with during their childhoods in Canada's Southern Ontario. In her teens, the enterprising Martha ran her own mini cottage industry, making and selling Barbie clothes for neighborhood kids.

Although Martha had many art skills, her greatest loves were costuming and puppetry, so after high school she decided to study technical theater, hoping to become a costume designer. After one year at Ryerson Polytechnical Institute in Toronto, she left, got married and became a "stay-at-home" mom. But she never surrendered her dreams of costuming. In her spare time she made costume dolls to enter in fairs and competitions, winning virtually every first place ribbon for several years running. She eventually went into business making fabric dolls with molded-cloth faces. These proved to be popular and business was good…too good. She was so busy filling orders that her foot was constantly to the sewing machine pedal, causing her to tear the ligaments in her heel. "Well, there went the whole cloth-doll business!" Martha says. "However, never being one to sit still long, I used this time to experiment with new mediums and to make things for myself. I had been frustrated for some time with the limitations of the fabric dolls, and after discovering Super Sculpey, set about trying to create more realistic adult figures, mostly fantasy types."

By this time Marianne had graduated with honors from Sheridan College, where she studied technical illustration, and was working as a computer graphics artist. Watching her big sister sculpt, Marianne wanted to try her hand at it, too. Occasionally she would sketch a figure, sculpt a head, and then pass it on to Martha, who would sculpt the hands and make the rest of the figure based on Marianne's drawing.

Working in this vein, the two sisters experimented for several years, making figures for themselves as well as for a few collectors. Finally in 1993, the pair felt ready to offer their work for sale and attended their first doll show

with their new sculpted dolls. They've never looked back. Since that time, Marianne has done almost all the sculpting, and Martha has done all the costumes and finishing.

Today Martha and Marianne are best known for their realistic historical figures and fantasy creations, one-of-a-kind dolls that are usually eighteen inches high and sell for up to $4,000 each. The sisters do, however, occasionally venture out into new frontiers. "The ethnic figures come along when I feel the need to try something new to sculpt," Marianne notes. "I have a reference folder with many ethnic faces, and I go through it and find a face that speaks to me. After making it, I leave it to Martha to figure out how to dress it."

"The Moor" is an early example of the sisters' efforts at black portrayal. The eighteen-inch piece, which is made of Super Sculpey with a soft body over a wire armature, is the very first black face—either male or female—that Marianne sculpted. Inspired by Billy Dee Williams, the doll has eyes that are painted, as is all of its facial hair. Marianne sculpted the features—as she does with most of her faces—by working from photographs. "If an artist does not do this, all his work tends to look the same, since an artist unconsciously puts his own eyes and mouth on any figure he sculpts," she explains. "So, in order to make a figure not look like ourselves, or our relatives, it is important to follow a photo. This is especially true when doing ethnic figures. Facial structures and bones are different in blacks and whites. You can't just fill a porcelain mold with brown slip, and then call it a black doll. The faces are very different, and one needs to pay attention to the details."

The particulars of the costuming were up to Martha. She went to town creating his colorful outfit. "The Moor" makes a dashing figure dressed in silks and fancy brocade for his vest, with lots of fringe and gold beads added for extra dazzle.

"I have a huge stash of fabrics, and among them are some very beautiful, colorful, exotic materials," says Martha with obvious relish. "These don't really work well on 'white' characters. We need someone more exotic."

Handsome, colorful, virile and with a hint of the scoundrel, "The Moor" fits the description. He's definitely a lady's man made to suit these two ladies.

*"The Moor," 18 inches, Super Sculpey with a soft body over a wire armature*

# ANNA ABIGAIL BRAHMS

*"With profound beauty, Abigail uses her intuitive power to liberate the heart and soul of her dolls. They are a testimony to the richness of her creative ability. You cannot help feeling that each doll was created exclusively for you."—BAW*

Anna Abigail Brahms, who started out to be a sculptor working in wood and marble, came to dollmaking through a series of circumstances. Born in Jerusalem, she studied art history at the University of Jerusalem in Israel. After graduating, she worked for a television station designing scenery. Asked to make a hand puppet for one of the TV shows, she constructed a "Snow Queen" from papier-mâché. She enjoyed the process so much that she joined a puppet theater in Tel Aviv. Called upon to be a woman-of-all-trades at the small theater company, she was soon adept at making marionettes and rod puppets. From there it was a natural progression to dollmaking.

She made her first doll in 1974. Just a year later, she was asked to exhibit some of her large wooden dolls—many of them of ethnic subjects—at the Museum of the City of Jerusalem. In 1980, Thomas Boland, an influential artists' representative, agreed to add her to his slate of artists; he introduced her work to a wider, more sophisticated sphere of American and international doll connoisseurs and enthusiasts.

The shy, reticent woman, whom noted doll critics have called "the pioneer in the field of the contemporary artist," was soon making waves with her realistic pieces that truly were more art than playthings. Throughout her long and influential career, Brahms has consistently given the world figurative poems of love and beauty, direct from her heart to those of her collectors. Today, working from the cozy sanctuary of her home studio in a small rural part of Massachusetts, she still prefers to let her dolls speak for her. "I am an observer. I love people but I am shy. I express my love through my art. I do hope that my dolls will 'speak' to others and give them some comfort."

Making up to nineteen one-of-a-kind dolls a year, Brahms likes to work in wood to create her larger, more statuesque dolls, and Fimo for her smaller, more delicate pieces. Using old photographs as reference material, she makes dolls that range in size from sixteen to thirty inches, and in price from $5,000 to $7,000.

A significant number of her dolls have been of black characters. "I'm always interested in portraying a psychological portrait. While I like the natural elegance and grace of black dolls' features, I am less concerned about the clothes or of achieving 'perfect' features. With my

*"Young Woman with Red Shawl,"*
*18 inches (seated), Fimo*

black dolls I find I often want to reveal the inner life, to show figures of quiet strength and dignity. It's the inner spirit, the emotional state of the subject, that compels me most."

An excellent example of Brahms' skill at depicting blacks is the doll she created specifically for this book. Brahms, who doesn't name her dolls ("In this way they fully belong to the person who purchased them," she explains), titled the piece "Young Woman with Red Shawl." Priced at $6,600, the one-of-kind piece was inspired by Sojourner Truth (1797-1883), the ex-slave who became a noted abolitionist, women's rights advocate and preacher. "She was fierce and powerful, and a great speaker," says Brahms.

# UTA BRAUSER

*'Uta's dolls capture the excitement of urban youth and the 'coolness' of their attitude. They celebrate a new generation of sensational dolls, each with a persona that stands out from the competition."—BAW*

Uta Brauser's black dolls would definitely find themselves at home in the 'hood. Although it's an environment the artist herself feels equally at ease in, it's a long way from her original European roots.

Born in 1963, in Munich, Germany, the artist was inspired by her mother, a portrait painter, to follow her artistic impulses early on through painting and sculpting. "I've been working with dolls and portraits since I was a teenager. I was doing caricatures of specific people as gifts, but I did them as marionettes. I did some of my teachers," Brauser reminisces, adding with obvious relish, "that made them angry."

In 1984, shortly after graduating from her studies, the adventurous and rebellious young woman moved to Italy. "I fell in love with the country, at first the southern part, then Florence. Wherever I lived I found the necessary resources to make my art happen. Florence has a great selection of crafts and manufacturing industries, so that was a definite plus," says Brauser, who lived in Italy for ten years before moving to New York in search of new inspirations.

"I wanted to do portraits of beautiful people, and I saw beautiful people on the streets of New York," Brauser notes. "I loved seeing the variety of skin colors and the clothing. I am inspired by personalities, fashion and philosophical statements, and in New York there is all this and so much more."

*"Fly Girl," 4 inches, resin (Photo: Richard Mitchell); Opposite page: "Girl Princesses," 23 inches, ceramic*

The theater of the New York streets provided Brauser with a never-ending cast of characters. A reflection of city life during the late 1980s and early 1990s, when the new wave of African-American pride was cresting, Brauser's Streetkids series allowed the artist to make many statements—about people, fashion and politics. "I found a lot of inspiration in the New York kids' society with its multicultural mix; they were a funky crowd of creative individuals with the awareness of a new-thinking generation," the artist explains.

Brauser eagerly embraced this new-thinking philosophy, applying it to her own creative style and methodology. "I developed my technique of acrylic on ceramic because I discovered that this was my best form of artistic expression. Since 1986 I decided that I do not need to fit into doll collecting's typical standards—i.e. the tendency to use porcelain for everything. I felt that porcelain is naturally too shiny and white in base, and when you color a porcelain slip, it always has a gray tone. I found this unfit for the beauty and texture of brown skin tones. So I went with ceramic and acrylic. I've always explained to the buyer 'the piece of art you are buying goes on the wall or on a cabinet; it does not need to be dishwasher-proof!'" says the artist, who is often as noteworthy for her flamboyant personal style and outspoken views as for her art.

Brauser's distinctive dolls are all one-of-a-kind pieces. Although taken from the same mold, each piece is individually costumed and painted. She sculpts the body, then makes a casting mold. Once she has the basic model, the individual dolls are honed so that no two have the same facial expression. The dolls, which are from eight to eighteen inches in height, sell for about $400 to $2,000. Although her choice of subjects is far-ranging—she's created everything from marionettes and court jesters to Renaissance ladies and baby dolls—her most striking and controversial pieces are her contemporary renderings of African-American adolescents and teens.

"I have long been an admirer of black Americans," Brauser explains. "I find them beautiful and wanted to do sculptures or portraits of them, but I never really was convinced I could do this because I am white and a foreigner. When I started making black dolls, most of them were men. Then, shortly after I came out with the male dolls, I developed, based on requests from collectors, an entire line of children and women to have a complete community."

Now a single mother, Brauser is ready to embark on another stage of her personal and artist life. After ten years of New York City living, she has moved with her four-year-old son, Ezra Achim, to Madrid, New Mexico. "To survive as a single parent with a very lively, high-energy child in the city is so hard," she explains. "And

September 11 added a major health hazard and even more pressure on us when my child started becoming constantly sick with coughs, asthma and flu-type symptoms. I realized that if I took him out of New York City, he would be fine. I always planned to be in a gorgeous country area if I ever had to leave the city. Upstate New York just does not compare with the beauty and sunshine over here. New Mexico has the same tempting, life-sweetening sunshine as Italy. Now I am closer to the earth in New Mexico and I will build a clay house (here called adobe) after the African models.

"The community I've found is also very special and inspiring," Brauser notes. "We are a fun artists' town of creative people, alternative thinkers and alternative power sources. It's a simple life, no corporate madness; it's perfect for a kid."

It's also seemingly ideal for working. Indeed, Brauser is full of plans: "I am going to work more with busts and full sculpts. I will still make dolls, but not as many. Clay has always been my main passion, and I live in the land of clay now."

*Below: "Kid Phat," 8½ inches, resin; Opposite page: "Dr. Smooth," 9 inches, resin (Photos: Richard Mitchell)*

# BARBARA THIERY BUYSSE

*"Barbara's artistic ability is delicately expressed in her wonderful hand-painted cloth dolls dressed in vintage fabrics. She imparts so much power and passion to her dolls that they seem to speak. Her dolls will surely be cherished for generations."—BAW*

The simplicity and "homey" appeal of Barbara Thiery Buysse's dolls cajole their way into your heart almost without you realizing it. Her cloth dolls, with their primitive hand-painted features and soft huggable qualities, have a surprisingly lifelike nature thanks to the artist's signature style—imbuing her dolls' flat faces with a three-dimensional quality through the skillful layering of paint.

Buysse is a painter by training. As a child, she attended the Art Institute of Chicago until 1964, when she went on to study in the art department of Western Michigan University; however, she earned a Bachelor of Arts degree in psychology in 1978 from William James College. She was able to join both endeavors when she began to work as an art therapist and counselor at a facility for outpatients and a halfway house for troubled youth. There, in an attempt to draw out her young patients, she started to sketch their portraits, offering the drawings to them at the end of their sessions.

Buysse carried portrait drawing a step further when, in 1977, she began making dolls with painted faces. "I've always had an interest in the cloth doll and was well acquainted with American dolls like the 'Columbian' by Emma Adams and Martha Chase, but I was also fond of any painted rag doll I came across. To simply sew up a cloth form and paint or draw an effigy upon that surface always seemed the essence of form and play. To me, cloth has a pliable, immediate and tactile nature."

Buysse tried to sell her creations—all oil painted on a flat cloth surface—but did not encounter much interest. "There was not the fever for handmade, which has now come into its own. Somehow, the plain cloth doll was a poor cousin to bisque, porcelain and other materials. When I started making dolls again in the 1980s, I began with a black doll. I started painting the black children that I saw in family therapy. About this time I was also reading black authors, such as Toni Morrison and Maya Angelou, and many of my dolls were inspired by their characters," says Buysse who notes that seventy-five-percent of her dolls are of color, almost all of them black.

"I have often been asked why I've chosen to work in

*Right: "Conjurer," 25 inches, oil on cloth;*
*Opposite page: "Daisy," 15 inches, cloth*

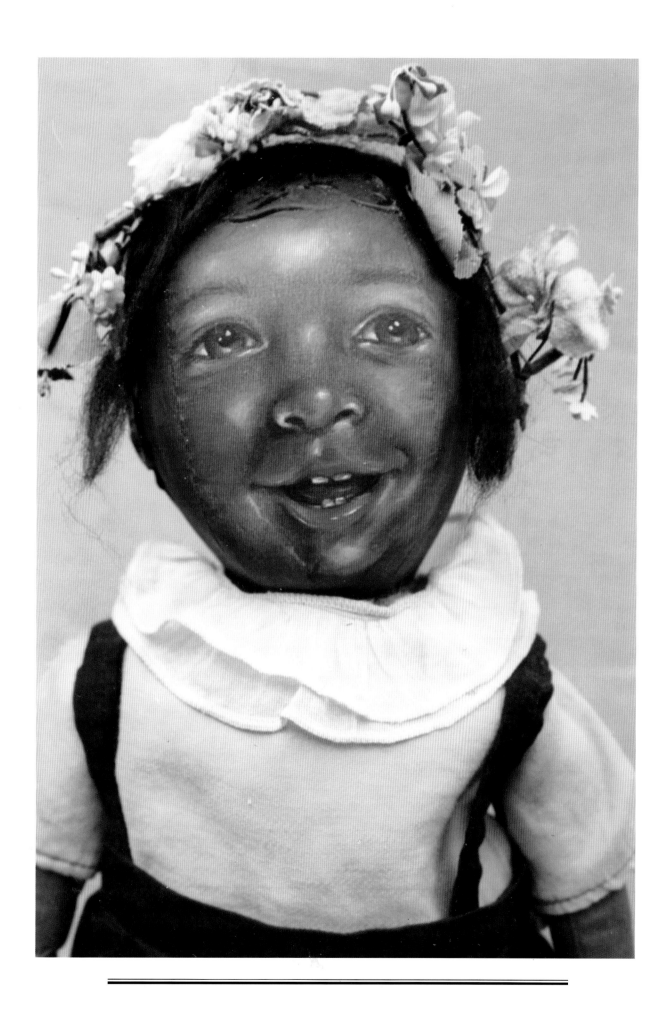

*Above: "Celia," 25 inches, oil on cloth;*
*Left: Untitled, 15 inches, oil on cloth*

black characters," she comments. "In fact, I have sometimes been criticized for this by black women, because they feel I am usurping or riding on the coattails of their culture, and on occasion by white women who think I must have a hang-up. Neither is true. As explanation, let me say this: I am part of a book group that meets regularly with an African-American book group to discuss books that reflect our cultures. What I have reaffirmed time and again is that we must enter into one another's experience before we can 'get it.' Whether it's in studying my black friends or the families I saw professionally, the range of features, skin tones and hair coloring of African Americans has always struck me. Oh, those skin tones! I paint in oils much in the technique of the Old Masters—layering many thin glazes to achieve a depth, a life beneath the surface. The African-American faces I've done lend themselves to that particular glow."

Buysse's dolls also tend to reflect the artist's preference for the antique. "They are frequently dressed in antique materials," she explains, "and if I use a new fabric, I comb it with a wire brush to raise the threads and soften it. But though I may be in the tradition of the eighteenth- and nineteenth-century dollmaker, my dolls do not perpetuate the stereotype of the black faces with round white eyes, which relegate a people to cartoon status. I believe each of my faces speaks for its humanity and dignity."

Buysse, who made most of her dolls in the 1990s, doesn't do as many now, creating them only as inspiration strikes her or upon special requests. Named Johnna Art Dolls after her oldest daughter, Buysse's dolls range in size from eight to twenty-five inches and are priced from $350 to $800.

The faces of Buysse's dolls bear special scrutiny. "I believe I was one of the first to revive the old tradition of painting on simple form, because that's what I wanted to look at, but couldn't afford the antique pieces. I am intrigued—almost plagued—by the human face in all its incarnations. As the poet Rumi has said, 'To look, to really look, is to understand.'"

# JENNIFER CANTON

*"Jennifer's artistry is inspiring, sublimely rich in spirit. Her dolls evoke fond memories of the past. They are astonishing detailed, with emotion, while interpreting a history of a people with dignity and truth."—BAW*

A Virginian born and bred, Jennifer Canton's earliest memories revolve around a love of animals and the outdoors, which likely explains why her earliest works reflected these themes. Starting out as a hobbyist working in oils, acrylics and textiles, she began participating in local art shows in the early 1970s, while also sharpening her graphic design skills as a freelance advertising artist.

"I had my hands in every artist's medium, from fashion design and sewing for myself and my girls, to papermaking, painting, calligraphy, printmaking and all sorts of crafts," she relates. "I was spinning in a circle, not seeing to advance in any one direction and knowing there was something else that I was supposed to do. I sat down, and literally asked God to give me one thing to do—and to make it apparent to me, quickly!"

Canton's prayers were answered. In 1991, she made her first polymer clay figure—a mother rabbit holding her litter of bunnies—as a present for her mother. Other similar creatures followed. "Bunnies, rats and mice infested every nook. My husband then challenged me to make a human likeness. What followed was a por-

*"The Givers, Part I," 14 inches, Super Sculpey*

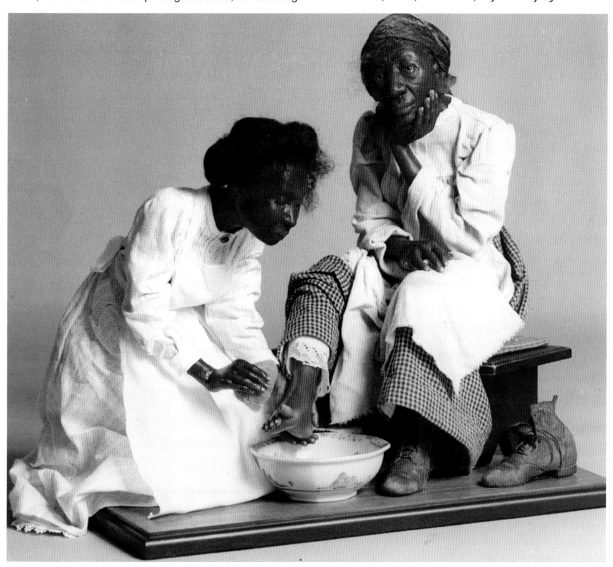

43

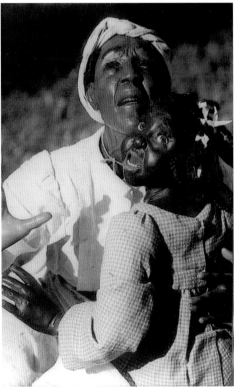

*Above: "Oh, Mary—Don't You Cry!"*
*14 inches, Cernit and Super Sculpey;*
*Left: "Tree of Life," 21 inches, Cernit and*
*Super Sculpey*

trait of my great-grandmother, Ida Scott, as I remembered her from my childhood. Thereafter, the animals became infrequent visitors to my workbench. As my confidence grew and I stretched my abilities, the clay became more than a vehicle for my imagination. The issue of slavery in our country's past has always intrigued me. Having read volumes of the slave narratives collected during the Federal Writers' Folklore Project of the 1920s and 1930s, I began to create likenesses of the women and children that spoke to me from those pages. I would say that for several years now, the major body of my work—about ninety percent—has been devoted to these voices.

"Surrounded by the heritage and stories of the Old South, I have always been drawn to the dark issue of

slavery. The stories I have read and heard over my lifetime have impacted me emotionally because they come from a time—and a mind-frame—so culturally removed from my own. It is my desire that when someone views my work, they will be drawn into the scene, absorbed by the eyes and what the hands are doing. I want the viewer to know the strength, the lasting hope, the endurance of these very real people from our past. I am awed by the kind of physical, emotional and spiritual fortitude a people must have had to have endured a life not their own."

Creating six to ten major works a year, Canton never lacks for inspiration. "Each of my black portraits is a personality that is tugging at my heart to be born in the clay. I strive for absolute realism. The eyes, first, must be a silent testament to the pain, joy, love, fear and other

*"I've Known Rivers," 12 inches, Super Sculpey*

emotion the character is communicating. Even more, I feel that the hands and feet must mirror the soul. The clothes, typically antique silks and cottons, must look truly worn; the soles of the feet and the capable hands, used," says Canton of her mostly one-of-a-kinds, which are priced from $75 to $4,200 and stand twelve to twenty-one inches high.

Canton has had very little formal art training. She briefly attended the York Academy of Applied Art in York, Pennsylvania, before going on to work as a staff artist at a newspaper. Eventually, she freelanced from home for advertising agencies. While living in Orlando, Florida, she joined a local original doll artists' group, through which she grew increasingly aware of the world of doll art. And the world of doll art became increasingly aware of her as her work began appearing in the pages of doll publications and winning awards. However, her artistic pursuits were put on hold when she and her family moved from Florida to Virginia's Shenandoah Valley. "Upon my husband's semi-retirement from medical practice, we purchased a small farm, enabling my equine interests to literally take over every spare moment of my life," Canton says of her three-year hiatus from creating her characters.

Ironically, a dramatic sporting accident, which left her paralyzed, marked her return to sculpting. "Everything can change in the blink of an eye. I had started out for an afternoon of foxhunting on my beloved horse, Stoli, who is bold and brave, but had never before run to hounds. It was a small field and, about a half-hour into the hunt, I remember counting up to a fence, thinking what a wonderful time I was having. My next memory was of being air-evacuated to the University of Virginia Medical Center in Charlottesville. Days later I awoke, paralyzed on my right side from a spinal cord injury and a broken neck. I also suffered a broken shoulder, scapula, eleven shattered ribs, a punctured lung and other minor injuries.

"My recovery has been slow and painful, but miraculously, almost complete now. Through this experience, I have realized that it is important to achieve balance and to exercise those gifts that have been given to us. Early in my recovery, I feared that I would never have enough control over my right side to be able to sculpt again. I was given a rubber ball to squeeze, but I demanded clay. I was fortunate that I only bruised my spinal cord. I regained feeling and control, and began sculpting again within four months. I have learned that balance is more than a good seat and good legs over fences; it is an awareness of one's responsibility to self and family and purpose in life. It is my belief that my ability to sculpt is a direct gift from God and what gives my work its 'soul.'"

# ROSIE CHAPMAN

*"Rosie believes creativity is a responsibility and visual interpretation is everything. Her doll treasures, designed with you in mind—from the very first stitch to the last accentuating detail—are unforgettable."—BAW*

**I** was never artistic before I started making dolls. As a matter of fact, I never really had much interest in dolls until I started making them myself. Now I wish more women would go back to 'playing with dolls' again," says Rosie Chapman, a.k.a. Miz Rosie. "It is therapeutic, relaxing and gratifying."

Miz Rosie ought to know. She began making dolls ten years ago as a form of therapy. "I survived two major surgeries within a month of each other; the second surgery was cancer-related," she says. "I suffered from post-traumatic stress disorder a few months after the surgery due to an accident at work. So, I began making African-American Raggedy Ann and Andy dolls dressed in bright colors and African fabrics. When I grew bored with them six months later, I started sculpting dolls in polymer clay. I used magazines and books to teach myself how to sculpt. After a year of struggling on my own, I traveled all over the country to take doll classes. I continue taking them today to learn new methods and improve my skills."

The dollmaker, who has a master's degree in social work and is now working towards a master's degree in art, has created dolls made of cloth, fiber, polymer clay, paper clay, metal and wood. "I most enjoy working in fiber because of all the textures, designs and colors that are available. I also love working in paper-clay and polymer clay because with them I can sculpt faces and body parts in the likeness of people."

Miz Rosie sculpts about 100 dolls a year. She creates one-of-a-kind pieces, as well as limited editions of ten or less. Varying in height from eight inches to five feet, her dolls sell for $75 to $1,500. Originally, she notes, almost all of her pieces represented black characters, but "now I'm more diversified. About seventy-five percent of my dolls are African or African American, and the other twenty-five percent are made up of Eurasian, Hispanic, Native American and Oriental. What attracts me to portraying blacks is the beauty of my heritage and the pride I have in my own people.

"I dream much of what I do, and I use life's experiences, magazine pictures, artist renditions and family members as subjects," says Miz Rosie, who describes her artistic style as spirit-fueled, soulful and moving. "My dolls have been known to speak to people. Their eyes tell stories. I love to see people laugh, cry or just sigh when they look at my work! I want them to truly feel the spirit of the doll and the messages I tried to relay when I created them."

When one looks at a work like "Grandma Clara" the viewer can feel the love Miz Rosie had for this special woman in her life. "My grandmother Clara Gilmore died a few days before Christmas, and my doll was made a few months later, during my grieving period," the artist explains.

Just as engaging, but totally different in its upbeat, whimsical quality, is her "Giggling Guardian Angel"; it came as a vision in the night. "I dreamed I heard someone laughing and I saw a little angel who said, 'I'm giggling at all the dumb things you do.' It was 3 a.m., but I went into my studio and started making my first giggling angel. I know everybody else must

*"Giggling Guardian Angel,"*
*4 inches, polymer clay*

have one too." With "You're Never Too Old to Dance, Rosie Lee," Miz Rosie tells others—and herself—that there's always time to stretch your boundaries and develop your talents. "I started tap dance classes at the age of 48," says the energetic and enthusiastic Miz Rosie, who was born in 1950. "I had been inspired to take tap after seeing Savion Glover in *Bring in Da Noise, Bring in Da Funk*. Although it took me a year to get the hang of tap, I decided that 'you're never too old to dance' when I noticed that four of the people in my tap class were over sixty-five years old."

Yes, folks—make way for Miz Rosie and her dolls; they're steppin' on up!

*Below: "Grandma Clara," 21 inches, paperclay covered with cloth; Right: "You're Never Too Old to Dance, Rosie Lee," 18 inches, doe suede fabric*

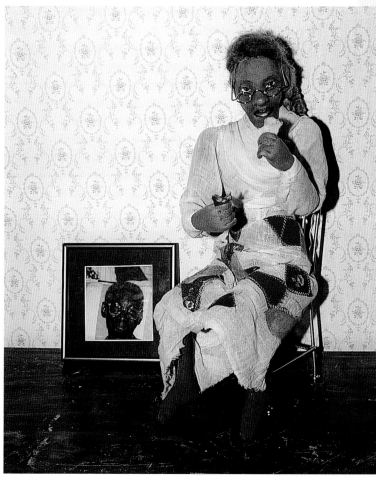

# PATRICIA COLEMAN~COBB

*"Pat is a fabulous doll artist, a master of capturing cultural reflection. Her dolls are uniquely and distinctively different, designed to speak your language. Imbued with liveliness and character, these personalities reflect happiness, motherhood and childhood remembrances."—BAW*

The designer and creator of The Cobblestone Collection, Patricia Coleman-Cobb is known for her handmade, cloth and clay sculptured dolls. The artist individually handcrafts every detail, particularly the dolls' clothing. "Having received my Bachelor of Science degree in clothing and textiles from Cheyney University, I am meticulous about the details," she notes. "Besides the emotional appeal, this is one of the aspects of my work that truly stands out. Collectors often comment on the construction and design of my characters' clothing, going as far as asking me to do those same designs for them! I spend a lot of time making sure that the inside of the garment looks as well as the outside of the piece."

Coleman-Cobb's dolls have earned several local and national awards, and her work has been featured in numerous publications, including Susanna Oroyan's *Anatomy of a Doll*. In addition, for two consecutive years, her work was chosen to be included as part of a yearlong traveling exhibit called "The Figure in Cloth."

The Philadelphia native taught at The Art Institute of Philadelphia for twelve years, until her recent relocation to the Atlanta area, where she now lives with her husband, Larry G. Cobb, an attorney, and their three sons. Coleman-Cobb has just written her first book, titled *Angels in the Mud*, which she describes as a "soulful voyage intertwining my life and my art through pictures and stories that caress the mind and soothe the spirit."

Dolls entered Coleman-Cobb's world ten years ago. "Late one night, after everyone else was in bed and the house was silent and still, I sat folding diapers and towels at the dining room table underneath the chandelier," she relates. "As I reached to pick up a towel, I noticed that, like faces in the clouds, the folds of laundry had personalities all their own. As I began to fumble and play with these shapes and expressions, I found myself laughing and talking aloud to myself about how this one looked like it was saying or doing one thing or another. One could have argued that I was delirious from a lack of sleep brought on by having two babies in diapers at the same time. But the next morning I got up, and drew and sewed the images that I remembered from the night before. Within six weeks, I was exhibiting at my first doll show, Dark Images, which is the largest black doll show on the East Coast.

"Before that night, I knew absolutely nothing about doll artistry. There were no special preparations or premonitions. But I look back on that moment with warmth and humility. Because right there in the still of the night, I was handed this amazing gift. It was like being touched by an angel. I have been designing dolls from that day on. And even though my designs have grown and expanded, my most notable pieces have been the simple designs of the original dolls that came to me that night."

The artist, who creates mostly one-of-a-kinds or small-number editions, works in cloth and polymer clays; her pieces are about twenty-two inches high. "My favorite technique is when I use the cloth as a skin over polymer clay to give a very realistic look and feel to my work," she notes. "I transfer the essence of my heart and

*"Pretty in Pink," 24 inches, cloth with a Super Sculpey mask*

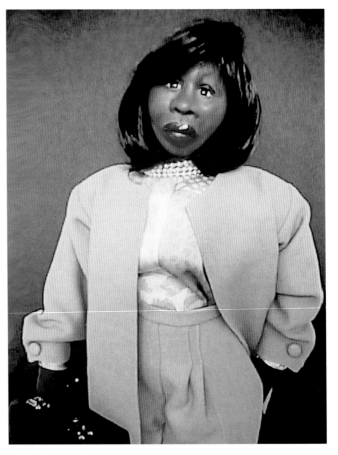

soul into all of my characters to give them depth and the positive spirit I carry within me. That often translates into collectors commenting on how much my art looks like me."

Coleman-Cobb imbues traditional styles and characters with her own signature brand of contemporary, urban earthiness. "I approach all of my subjects in the same manner that I approach life—with open-mindedness, respect and a willingness to learn. While it is important to have the basic techniques down, it is even more vital to be able to capture the spirit and the essence of the piece. When you look at my work, I don't want you to see it in fragments and say, 'Oh my, the eyes are perfect; the nose is proportioned exactly right; and the lips are precisely pouty.' I want the viewer to take in the whole experience. I have accomplished my goal when someone stops and says, 'Ooooh chil', look at you!' and then goes on to say, 'she looks like she's saying…' Attaining this goal is unexplainable; I kind of let go and watch as my hands get busy doing their thing.

"The most enjoyable part of my art is when the magic begins," she continues in an enthusiastic rush. "This is the part where God's wonderful gift to me truly kicks in. I realize it is happening when the work becomes somewhat effortless and the piece evolves into a separate entity wherein it is no longer necessary for me as the artist to have absolute control because the character's personality dictates my every move."

*Above right: "Herlena," 25 inches, seated, cloth covered with Super Sculpey mask; Above: "Loretta," 24 inches, cloth covered with Super Sculpey mask; Right: "Lillian," 27 inches, cloth covered with Super Sculpey mask*

# RICHARD AND JODI CREAGER

*"We are always astonished and delighted when these two highly creative persons blend their talents to express themselves through dolls. We are caught off guard because their unique creations are so consistently wonderful, flawlessly sculptured and unsurpassed in details. Each story the Creagers tell, each vignette they design, allows us to rejoice and share in their art."—BAW*

Like any great husband-and-wife team, Richard and Jodi Creager are two passionate individuals who bring their unique strengths and skills to collaborate as one in achieving a common goal. Their recipe for professional success: taking a little of each of their visions and seamlessly blending them to make powerful, moving statements with their extraordinary dolls.

It's a marriage made in doll heaven. After the couple has conceptualized and designed a piece, Jodi, who has enjoyed drawing and painting since she was a child, goes on to concentrate on sculpting the head and hands, constructing the body trunk, painting the doll, and costuming and wigging. Richard, who has worked as a machinist, mechanic, photographer, artist and teacher, focuses on sculpting the legs and feet, as well as constructing the footwear and other accessories and props. (His degree in industrial photography also comes in handy in photographing the dolls.)

Richard and Jodi, who wed in 1975, have been designing dolls together since 1979. They experimented with various mediums and began to steadily and surely build a name and reputation. In 1991, they were elected into the National Institute of American Doll Artists (NIADA), and by 1997, fitness guru and doll collector Richard Simmons had enlisted them to create resin elves and plush bears for the Goebel-produced Richard Simmons Collection of the Masters. On their own, they produce approximately fifteen dolls a year; prices for their one-of-a-kind pieces are typically in the $2,000 range.

Sharing a love of history, and studying the customs and traditions of various ethnic groups—with black characters figuring prominently among them—-have fueled their creativity, giving rise to many of their most memorable subjects.

"What identifies a doll as a work of art is its ability to project a human emotion to the viewer. It is this ability that will transcend time and allow a person in some future generation to view the work and feel what the artist felt at the moment of its creation," Richard notes. "As the character develops, we become emotionally involved in the life and story we have created for each piece. Knowing the character inside and out helps to breathe life into the doll."

With "Herero Woman," a one-of-a-kind piece that depicts a woman of the Herero tribe in her wedding

*Above: "Sunshine," 11 inches, polymer clay with a cloth body; Opposite page: "Grandpa's Surprise," 15 inches, polymer clay*

50

dress, the Creagers sought to bring out the power and thought behind the individual while simultaneously portraying the simple yet intricate details of the tribe's wedding ritual. Inspired by a photo that moved them, "Fulani," another one-of-a-kind, celebrates the universal interaction and interdependence between mother, child and animal.

"I think we look more to relationships and interaction than we do to the color of the doll we are portraying," Richard says. To prove it, they point to "Grandpa's Surprise." "In truth, this piece could have been created in any ethnicity. But in our work, it usually takes one spark to ignite our creative flow. We saw a movie with Morgan Freeman, and his face is the gentlest face we have ever seen. From picturing his face, the characters were born." From there, they built upon Jodi's fond childhood memories of poking her nose in her grandpa's garage to see what "swell stuff" he was building. "Grandparents are just the best people," Jodi says. "Where would we be without them! We wanted to take our childhood memories and convey them in this piece."

"We were able to create many specialized things to bring the story to life," Richard continues. "The little girl is sneaking to catch a 'peek' at what grandpa has been making, and that moment when she realizes it is for her…oh, joy!"

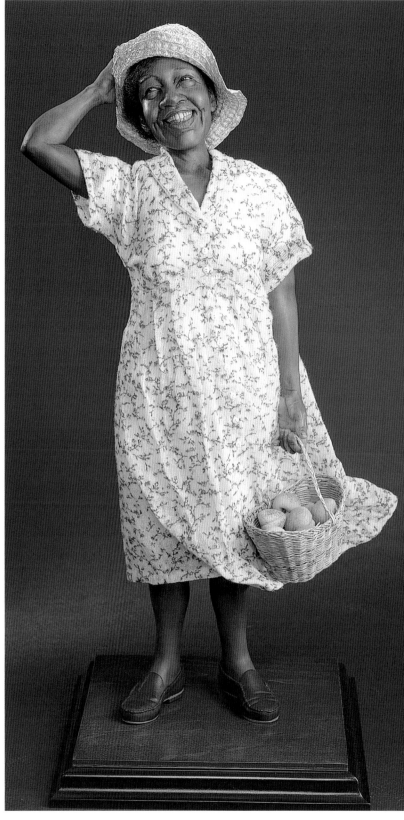

*Above: "Peaches," 16 inches, polymer clay with a cloth body; Left: "Herero Woman," 10 inches (seated), polymer clay; Opposite page: "Fulani," 15 inches, polymer clay*

# BRIGITTE DEVAL

*"Because her 'soul' is poured into each of her creations, Brigitte's dolls speak to us about enduring beauty and peace. Each doll has an unexplainable aura of purity and innocence."—BAW*

Considered by many as one of the top doll artists in the world, the German-born Brigitte Deval has been a doll lover—and dollmaker—since she was a child. Growing up exposed to the influence and example of her father, a famous portrait photographer, young Brigitte followed her own artistic impulses, making simple dolls modeled over bottles and sticks. As an adult, she first tried her hand at making puppets before moving on, in the late 1960s, to creating wax-over-ceramic dolls.

Deval's style is one of realistic beauty; her dolls, which run the gamut of humanity, all have thoughtful, soulful faces that speak to viewers, appealing to their emotions as well as their aesthetic appreciation. Deval creates striking, revealing portraits that noted doll critics have likened to the works of Francisco Goya and Thomas Gainsborough. Highly sought-after, her one-of-a-

kind dolls and small limited-edition pieces command prices that start at around $12,000 for the former and $5,000 for the latter. Most recently, she has started to create small angel ornaments that are more affordable at $500 to $700 each. Yet whether she is making one of her costly one-of-a-kinds or angelic cherubs, Deval invests all of her heart and artistry into every piece to create something that is individual and personal in nature. "All my pieces are different, even when they are editions," says the artist. "I normally work so free and do whatever I am feeling."

Her sources of inspiration are equally fluid and diverse. The artist, who has lived and worked in Italy since 1974 and is fluent in three languages, cites her multicultural heritage as a rich fountain of ideas and subject matter for her dolls, many of which are of ethnic characters.

Deval's dolls seem to speak on a much more fundamental and spiritual nature, making words unnecessary, even superfluous. Indeed, when asked to comment on why she is drawn to black characters, the soft-spoken artist finds it difficult to articulate her thoughts. "I'd need a very long time to think about this in order to give a 'good' answer," she apologizes. "I think it's a way to get closer to my subjects. I never had the opportunity to become close to someone who was black, so it brings me pleasure to produce, with only my imagination, black people as versions of myself." This potent attraction is one she's carried within her since a childhood experience.

"When I was a small child and going on a tramway," she relates, "I was close to a very dark African black man or woman—I can't remember what gender now—and it was very difficult for me to resist not touching the person's marvelous skin. I think this might have been my very first form of almost erotic feelings."

Alluring in a different way, "Heloise," which is part of a private collection, and "Fantasy Princess," made in 1999 and priced at $14,000, have a softness and innocence in their expressions that gently crooks a beckoning finger at the viewer, inviting him or her into the world behind their deep and soulful eyes.

*Left: "Fantasy Princess," 16 inches, white clay painted with acrylic color; Opposite page: "Heloise," 32 inches, white clay painted with acrylic color*

# TONIA MITCHELL FLOYD

*"Tonia's dolls are exciting and exquisitely designed. Made for your imagination, they invite you to join the artist in fantasyland. Just looking at these whimsical dolls, completed with myriad colors and fabrics, can bring happiness."—BAW*

The first thing one notices about Tonia Mitchell Floyd's dolls is the riot of color. Vibrant, chaotic, exuberant, they're a celebration. Forget shy and demure; her characters clamber for attention, engaging their viewers in a visceral, sensory connection. And the artist is every bit as distinctive as her dolls. This native Georgian with a wanderlust spirit is anything but your stereotypical business administration major (although that's what she graduated with from the University of Georgia). She thrives on thinking out of the box and going against type. From her travels and living-abroad experiences in Europe, Central America and Southeast Asia, she's come to develop a deep respect and appreciation for other cultures, and different ways of seeing the world and doing things. Through her work, she strives to communicate and share some of these life lessons.

"I came from a very traditional home; my mother was an educator, and my father was a military man, a pilot who retired as a general. To make them happy, I did what they expected of me," relates the artist, who labored for several years as one of America's corporate suits. "But it got to the point where I said to myself, 'You know what? I don't like this. I've fulfilled my commitments to my family. Now it's time to explore what I want.'"

After working for seven years at a home-based silk-screening business, Mitchell Floyd gave it up when she became pregnant. Life—by way of a husband, three sons and self-exploration—took center stage. Her gradual discovery of dollmaking was the result of a spiritual journey, which is still ongoing. "Through vivid revelations and a series of serendipitous events around 1994, I recognized my innate creative muse and embraced dollmaking as a medium of self-expression," the self-taught artist reveals. "I literally prayed for direction. I never really ever discovered dollmaking; we kind of recognized and embraced each other.

"Dollmaking is a fascinating artistic journey that celebrates the human spirit. I love every aspect of it. Dolls speak to my attraction for exploring various artistic techniques without being confined to one. Dollmaking involves designing, sewing, sculpting, painting, wigging, costuming and other skills," says the artist, who insists her only frustration is that "the endless creative possibilities outnumber the hours in a day."

*Above: "Madame Jubilee," 48 inches, resin and cloth; Opposite page: "Cousin Hattie Mae," 48 inches, resin and cloth*

Mitchell Floyd weaves her perceptions into captivating works of art that illustrate her intuitive knack for balancing colors, patterns and textures. Each of her dolls becomes an exercise in fine-tuning new concepts and designs.

Like the people they're inspired by, her characters come in all shapes and sizes. These enchanting fantasy figures are lovingly and painstakingly detailed with hand tinting and painting, and quirky embellishments to produce truly one-of-a-kind pieces.

Cloth is Mitchell Floyd's favorite medium. "It is colorful and textural with infinite patterns," says the artist, who has been making dolls for ten years. "I sew a piece of my spirit into each doll in hopes of evoking joy, as well as a majestic awareness of being one with the universe."

Mitchell Floyd's creations are primarily one-of-a-kind pieces. On occasion, she also makes commissioned limited editions of less than 100 pieces. Her characters generally range in price from $150 to $3,000. The size spectrum goes from five-inch dolls to life-sized figures measuring five feet. Most of her work deals with black subjects. "My heritage inspires my creation," the artist says simply. "The black experience is most familiar to me."

Mitchell Floyd's dolls are known for their caricature-like style and lighthearted whimsical flair. Her attention to detail and facial expressions also help put her distinctive stamp on everything she fashions. Her characters come to life with an exuberant mix of style and panache. They seem to grab at life with gusto and an appreciation that reflects their creator's own sensibilities.

"I'm pretty carefree," says Mitchell Floyd. "I live in a fantasy world where all things are possible. When I was a child I felt I could fly. I really thought that if I tried hard enough, I could leave the ground. Today, I realize that I can't literally fly, but I've never lost that sense that anything is possible if you wish it hard enough.

"People are so inhibited that they don't take chances," she says with quiet passion. "I'm thankful I've never lost my expectation of the joy of surprises. My dolls give me the power to create that feeling of wonderment and joy in everyday life. My dolls are little pieces of my imagination." They ferment those magical feelings that brew in all of us, allowing her—and the people who connect with her work—to open that heady bottle and become intoxicated with life's possibilities and pleasures.

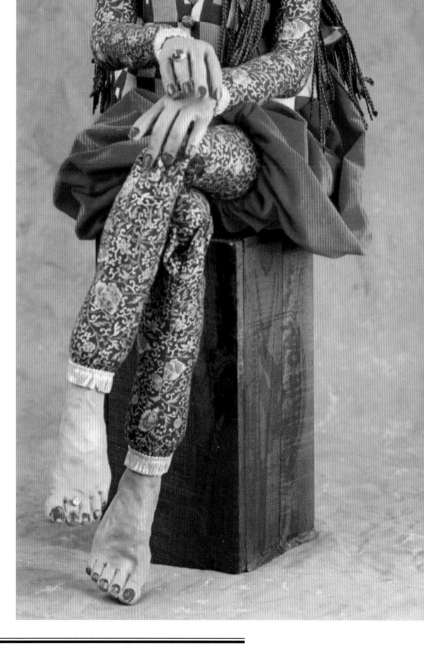

*Right: "Ishengahla," 18 inches, resin and cloth;*
*Opposite page: "Madame Mardi Gras,"*
*48 inches, resin and cloth*

# ELISSA GLASSGOLD

*"Ageless beauty and simplicity, the essence of life and a quiet spirit emanate from Elissa's dolls. Her children-in-miniature are exemplary works of art."—BAW*

**66** I was a doll-obsessed child," says Elissa Glassgold, who was born in 1950 in Detroit, Michigan. "My dolls meant the world to me. I wasn't a collector, though. I played with my dolls, and I definitely used them up. I sculpted little figures, made hand puppets, and drew pictures of children with dolls. I looked at all the cherubs at the art museum, and wished that they were my baby dolls. I loved the Della Robbia children the most. I wanted the beautiful and mysterious carved angels to have arms that moved, and when I saw some dressed as they would have been on a Saint's Day, I began to dream of owning one."

Glassgold has a Bachelor of Fine Arts degree from the University of the Arts in Philadelphia, Pennsylvania, a four-year certificate from The Pennsylvania Academy of the Fine Arts, and a Master of Fine Arts degree from the University of North Carolina. In addition, she has received teaching certification from The University of the Arts. From 1987 to 1996, she was a professor of painting and art history at Rutgers-Temple Universities and at the Hudsian School of Art in Philadelphia. Currently, in addition to teaching kindergarten through eighth grade, she is designing an art curriculum for a school in North Philadelphia and teaching continuing education classes in painting at a school administered by the Philadelphia Museum of Art.

"As a painting student in a fine arts program I was not thinking about doing commercial work, and dolls were definitely not in the realm of acceptable forms,"

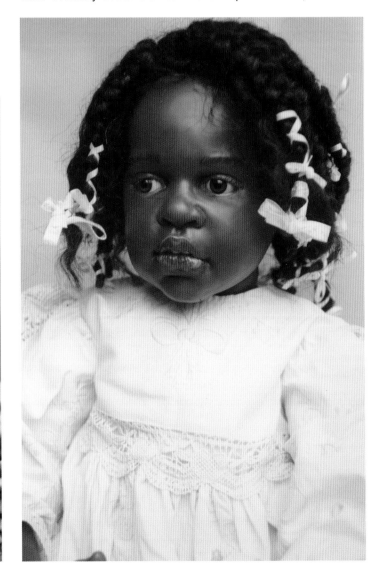

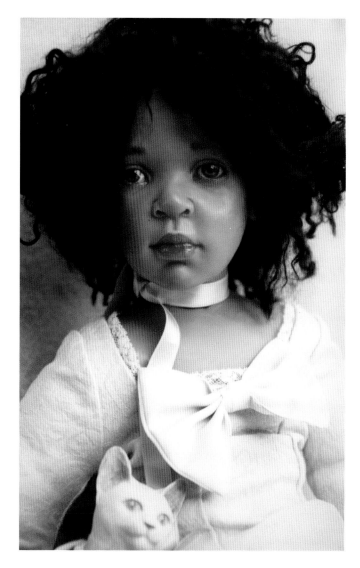

Glassgold notes. "It wasn't until I took my then three-year-old son to FAO Schwarz and saw Annette Himstedt's first dolls that I realized that doll design was a possibility. I began making 'real' dolls at that point, in 1990."

Glassgold started selling her dolls three years later. She's worked in hand-built stoneware and porcelain, cloth, Fimo, Cernit and cast resin. Her favorite material to date is resin, because it has the waxy, translucent look of Fimo or Cernit, but is more stable.

Currently Glassgold, who still paints and draws as well, is sculpting only about ten one-of-a-kind dolls a year. In the past, she created many more and annually produced about four of her designs in limited editions. She plans to create her own limited-edition dolls again, beginning in 2004. (Since 1999, Zapf Creation has been producing limited editions of her dolls. In fact, she considers her three ethnic dolls—one black, one Hispanic and one Asian—for Zapf's 2003 line to be the finest work she has done thus far.) Prices for her dolls range from $1,800 to $4,000 for one-of-a-kinds; $700 to $3,000 for limited-edition pieces; and $400 to $750 for vinyl dolls. Her dolls are large, ranging from eighteen to thirty-four inches.

The artist, who is best known for her portrayals of children, estimates that half of all her dolls are black. "The black dolls are simply a reflection of my own childhood, as I grew up in inner Detroit. The faces of my friends, classmates and neighbors happen easily for me, more than other ethnicities," says Glassgold, who adds that about a quarter of her dolls are of Asian children.

These days she has classrooms full of inspiration. "I'm memorizing and absorbing the faces of my students every day," Of "Child in Green Silk" Glassgold comments: "I was looking at a little girl who had these particularly highly defined features that made me think of the beauty she would turn into."

"Rachel" was also based on a student—"a second-grade student of mine, the only black child in the only suburban school I ever taught in. I had set out to produce a black doll, and there she was," Glassgold explains. "She was an artistic child, and there was a special recognition between us because of this. She was astounded when she saw the dolls."

The inspiration for "Cleofe" came from a novel by Joan Aiken. "The book was written for older children, and I was reading through the series with my son at the time. The story was about a group of kidnapped children held hostage by an evil queen, who used them to restore her youth. She dressed them as hand maidens and court children to keep them from appearing out of place, and therefore inviting suspicion. They were children from many countries, and I did a series of three. One was this doll, a child of color; the others were an Asian and a Caucasian child."

With her dolls—regardless of color or race—Glassgold invites the viewer to contemplate the mood of each particular piece, whether it be quiet, serious, reflective or in the process of breaking into a smiling face. "In this way one can feel an essence," she notes. "But is it the doll, or is it the viewer's feelings projected onto a sympathetic face?"

We leave it to the viewer to look at any of Glassgold's dolls and answer this question for him or herself.

*Above: "Cleofe," 34 inches, cast resin;*
*Opposite page, left: "Rachel," 30 inches, cast resin;*
*Far left: "Child in Green Silk," 27 inches, Fimo*

# HILDEGARD GÜNZEL

*"Hildegard Günzel is regarded as the doll artist's friend, held in the highest esteem by fellow dollmakers because of her willingness to teach and share. Out of her imagination, we receive dolls that are superbly sculptured and treasured for their warmness and innocence. Günzel's dolls allow us to enjoy and revisit childhood past."—BAW*

Chances are if you catch Hildegard Günzel at one of the many airports she frequents as part of her extensive business travels, she'll be studying everyone around her and happily sketching their faces. "I've found that the best times to observe people are when I am waiting for my flights," confides the world-renowned artist, who adds that American airports are the best places for spotting interesting black faces. "During my visits to the United States, I always study the beautiful black American children. The USA is a very interesting multicultural society and offers lots of opportunities to meet a wide facet of personalities. My drawing book is one of my most important companions when traveling there."

You might think the German artist—unquestionably one of the most talented, successful and beloved in the industry—would sit back and enjoy her well-earned fame and success. Not so. She seems happiest looking ahead in eager expectation of what's to come. Whether it's devising a secret formulation consisting of a special wax that gives her dolls a beautiful translucency, designing vinyl dolls for Götz, or founding her own doll museum featuring her work and that of other artists (which she did in 1996), Günzel's love of experimentation, curiosity and unbounded passion for creating dolls and, since 1996, teddy bears have kept her on the move creatively.

"I'm convinced that an artist should fight to progress in what he or she is doing," Günzel says. "I will never finish learning or stop looking at individuals, particularly children. In seeking to reflect the expressions on their faces, I never fail to be inspired."

It is this ever-constant striving to better herself and her art that has propelled Günzel to the upper echelon of the doll world. In an industry of many stellar talents, she stands apart. Many renowned doll artists have looked to her for knowledge and inspiration. Günzel has not disappointed. Through the issue of commercial molds (no longer available), dollmaking classes, instructional books and a video, she has generously shared her gifts with others, guiding and motivating by example. The dolls she's produced for her own business, The House of Günzel, and for other companies, such as Walterhauser Puppenmanufaktur and Götz Dolls, have

*Left: "Kyta," 35 inches, wax over porcelain; Opposite page: "Michelle," 30 inches, wax over porcelain*

earned her so many awards that she's lost count. Most recently, she received a Lifetime Achievement Award, presented to her in August of 2003 by the Iola, Wisconsin-based Jones Publishing, the owner of *DOLLS, Doll Crafter,* and *Doll Costuming* magazines.

It's been a long, heady trip since 1972, when she began making dolls as a hobby. "The first doll I created was for my son Kai, when he was one year old," she relates. "At this time there was nobody to learn from, so it was really learning by doing." She kept at it, and by 1977 had sold her first doll. With each doll she created she became more and more ensnared in the magical realm of fun and make-believe. That childlike enthusiasm couldn't help but spill over into the faces of her dolls, the overwhelming majority of which are children and babies. With their chubby faces and air of innocence, they're the promise of youth realized in porcelain.

Take, for example, her sweet-faced "Michelle." Part of the Born in the Winds of Time Millennium Collection of 2000, the doll is typical of her black pieces. Based on a real child, she represents, to Günzel, one of "today's children as they play with their fashion dolls." Günzel has made her engrossed in her own world where time does not pass. "It stands still, seeming to hold its breath, trying not to disturb the child's play. We adults can only watch quietly and for one magic moment, we are allowed to enjoy the extraordinary feeling that, even for us, time is forever."

With "Kyta," part of her 2002 Dreamweaver Collection, the artist wanted to give birth to her dreams. "In a way I am like a mother to my dolls. They are my creation, and like any mother, I want to give my children the best that I can. For their clothing, which I design myself, I use only the best materials: cashmere, silk and silk velvet. I search the world over for patterns that best suit the dolls I wish to create and that best reflect the image I have in my soul." Wearing a lace shirt, knitted bolero jacket, French dupioni silk skirt with large velvet bows, French silk pants and leather shoes with woven ribbons, and featuring a human-hair wig and blown-glass eyes, "Kyta" is indeed a vision taken form.

Hoping that all her dolls elicit love and respect, Günzel creates limited-edition and one-of-a-kind pieces, which command prices ranging from $5,000 to $14,000 for the former and from $15,000 to $40,000 for the latter. Günzel began sculpting in Cernit, but prefers plastiline today. All her finished dolls are of porcelain. She designs fifteen to twenty original dolls a year. Her limited-edition dolls run in edition sizes of twenty to twenty-five for distribution in America and twenty to twenty-five for Europe.

"Sometimes I feel that my dolls have made me give them a particular expression," says the artist. "It is as if they already know their look and character. At this great moment, I am always touched when we finally behold each other face to face."

# PHILIP HEATH

*"Philip Heath's dolls are exquisite masterpieces, filled with so much emotion and sensitivity. The artist is known for his propensity for personalization, and his reverence of children. Each doll has a distinct personality that touches all humanity in a celebration of life, making a lasting impression."—BAW*

"My life is one big crossroads! Always the unexpected comes up and takes me down another road," says Philip Heath. A quick review of his life proves the truth of this. The British-born Heath has been a teacher, a jewelry designer, a furniture designer and a world traveler, as well as having worked in the theatrical makeup and wardrobe trades. He came on the doll scene in 1985. His first porcelain pieces were created with his former wife, Christine. In 1989, the couple divorced, and he moved to Belgium, where he began making dolls on his own. In 1992, he started designing a line of vinyl dolls for the German-based Götz Dolls, an association he continued until he decided to take a break from the doll world in 1999.

In the fall of 2001, he returned from semi-retirement with the launch of his new company, Philip Heath Designs. Located in Valencia, Spain, Philip Health Designs creates lovely vinyl dolls in small limited editions, available for about $500 each.

"I have never been a patient man. I have always jumped rather than walked. I think I came to Valencia to learn patience. It is a great virtue and maybe if I had learned it earlier, I would have bypassed a lot of the pitfalls," says the artist. "I cannot predict the future, but presently feel content with my work. I'm full of ideas, and best of all, I'm producing my dolls exactly how I want to."

The personal satisfaction comes through in his professional efforts. Known and respected for his ravishingly beautiful and realistic portraits of children of color, Heath has rightfully earned the respect and admiration of his peers, collectors and the doll industry media.

"My art is the total concept that combines skills, intelligence and feelings to imbue an object with the ability to communicate," Heath notes. "My portraits speak for themselves." They do indeed. They also speak for the artist, as Heath acknowledges. "My work is like a mirror," he says. "It reflects my conflicts, my emotional state, sometimes too clearly, displaying more than I wish or even realize."

One thing that is crystal clear in his dolls, the majority of which deal with ethnic themes and subjects, is his deep love of and fascination with Africa and its many peoples. When he speaks of his experiences traveling through Africa, his face and voice come alive. "The color, heat, smell, noise, beauty, and most of all, the friendly children changed me dramatically," he exults. "I wanted to be black and beautiful, to carry myself elegantly and proudly. I immersed myself in their culture and lives. I fell in love with Africa!"

To Heath, tribes such as the Masai epitomize the poetic, sculptural ideals of beauty. They intrigue and excite him, fueling his inspiration and creative vision. "I believe the Masai to be one of the world's most beautiful people," he says, explaining how their gazelle-like bone structures, heavily lidded eyes, high cheekbones and exuberant mouths compel him to do their beauty justice with his sculptor's hands.

In order to capture their truest essence, Heath, who often works from photographs and memories of his subjects, immerses himself in the lives and nuances of his characters. When he speaks of his subjects it is with the

*Above: "Angel," 30 inches, vinyl;*
*Opposite page: "Jewel Lost," 33 inches, vinyl*

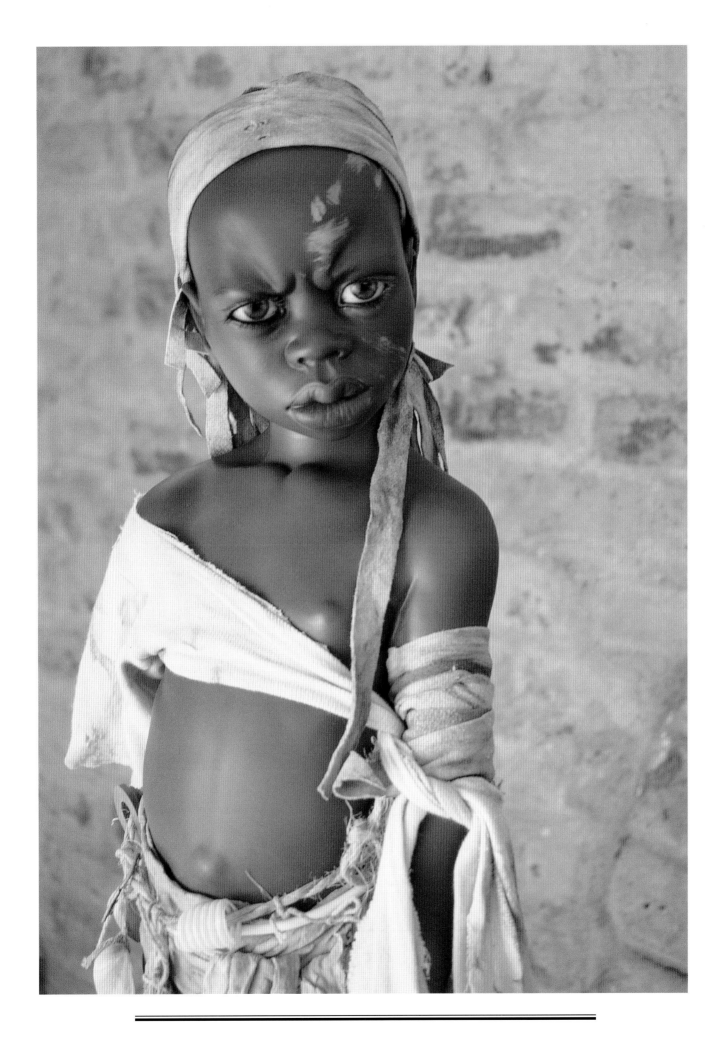

familiarity and warm affection of a lover who knows his beloved inside and out, and sees beyond the exterior to the potential locked within. Although his work is a clear vision of reality, at the same time, it is alive with the artist's hopeful idealism.

This contrasting duality is easy to observe in pieces such as "Jewel Lost" and "Jewel Found." "Jewel Lost" is a portrait of a girl from Zaire. "The original photos were sad and her physical condition distressing," Heath says. "I was so haunted by her expression of anger, tiredness and distress, that I collected shells, pretty pieces of glass, wood and sand softened by the waves and everything else I thought a child of her age would think pretty." With "Jewel Found" Heath takes the same portrait and re-interprets her with a brighter future. "Her hair has grown thick and luxuriant. Her cotton dress is decorated with beads," the artist explains. "The face is now clean, and the eyes are clear and alert. The only thing that remains is her anger and bad experiences that can't be washed away."

Just as immutable, Heath's own experiences have had a permanent effect on him and his work. "I think my love of the exotic, of travel, of ethnic peoples has made a sweeping difference in my work," Heath notes on the subject of what inspires him. That inspiration is alive and thriving today. From his new home base in sunny Spain, Heath happily continues to rediscover himself, and portray his personal and professional dimensions in his striking dolls of color that encompass and embrace his love of the exotic and beautiful.

# ANNETTE HIMSTEDT

*"Annette's dolls exemplify perfection in porcelain. Disarmingly beautiful, her dolls are so captivating and realistic. Pensive and subdued, each doll engages us with expressive moods and feeling."—BAW*

orn in Bad Lauchstädt, Germany, Annette Himstedt came to dollmaking via portraiture. "As a child I always loved drawing portraits," notes the self-taught artist. "Later I had the desire to transform these into three dimensions. Dolls were an obvious choice because they're based on human beings. In 1974, I started to make my first stone figures with pebbles. Later I made fabric dolls and eventually clay dolls. After a time, clay ceased to satisfy me as a material and I wanted to make porcelain dolls. In January of 1979, I took one of my clay dolls and drove to a nearby porcelain manufacturer. Despite having people patronize me— they thought I was just playing around— I met a mold maker there who ended up working with me for almost thirteen years."

Himstedt, who is nothing if not persistent, was determined to give reality to her vision. "I had always wanted to model children and set out to make dolls that were more realistic than any others that were around at that time. During the first few years of dollmaking I developed my own style and moved on from portraiture. It's always been important to me that my dolls look alive, convey character and warmth, and provoke feelings. I put a lot of myself into my 'Kinder' and I hope that collectors can sense this. It's also important to me that the faces leave enough room to reflect mood changes so they shift according to the way you feel when you look at them."

Through many years of financial, professional and emotional ups and downs Himstedt never lost sight of her goals or compromised her standards. In 1982, she sold her first porcelain doll, a one-of-a-kind piece; in 1986, she sold her first vinyl dolls. Today she has her own doll factory in Paderborn, Germany, where she employs a small group of key staff to produce her dolls— vinyl as well as porcelain—which are in high demand the

*"Khadiya," 24 inches, porcelain*

world over and have rightfully earned her much acclaim and many awards.

Although Himstedt has worked with fabric and clay, porcelain is without a doubt her forté. "It is like butter in my hands, and over the years I've developed a special technique, which enables me to work with porcelain from scratch without having to rely on other materials," she says. In recent years the artist has molded about twenty dolls per year. Most of these have been for her vinyl collection; three or four are for her porcelain Himstedt Masterpieces collection and about four dolls with carriages or prams are for her porcelain Himstedt Miniatures. Since 2002, she has extended her vinyl doll collections, for which she designs up to thirty-three different dolls. (She's kept the numbers the same for the Himstedt Masterpieces and Himstedt Miniatures.)

Himstedt bases her edition sizes on variables of her favorite numbers—seven and thirteen. "Either they are quite obviously contained in the number like 713 or they are hidden in the sum of digits like twenty-five or forty-three," she notes.

Himstedt Kinder dolls, which range in size from twenty-three to thirty inches, sell from $238 to $1,600. Prices for Himstedt Miniatures, which are from four to seven inches, go from $204 to $429. The Himstedt Masterpieces, about thirty inches tall, cost about $5,000.

Almost every collection she's made contains ethnic dolls. For her 2003 Himstedt Kinder collection, for instance, the artist created children representing different corners of the world. One of them is "Sveva," whose unusual facial expression particularly pleases Himstedt. "On one hand it seems to be very clear, yet it's also quite enigmatic and mysterious," she says, adding that

"Sveva" was inspired by a look back at a five-day trip to Senegal she embarked on for Unicef in 1985. (This journey also had inspired the creation of another earlier doll, "Fatou," which was part of the artist's 1986-87 collection.)

As Himstedt recalls, "It was a very unusual and adventurous trip. I was supposed to photograph children there and experience first-hand how they lived. We went to see the remotest villages, where time really seemed to have stood still. The local women weren't entitled to take part in any of the daily palaver, nor were the girls. They made a big exception for me only because I was accompanied by the local VSO (voluntary service overseas) worker. When I wanted to photograph the girls as well as the boys, no one there could understand it. For clothing for 'Fatou,' I had materials woven according to original African fabrics that I bought in a Senegalese village. I can still see the fabrics displayed, spread out on the dusty ground."

Whereas many of her dolls are based on real children, and the photographs and memories of them, other Himstedt creations are pure fantasy. For example, the graceful "Khadiya," from the 1996 Himstedt Masterpieces series, "is a product of my imagination," says the artist. "She comes from the Land of Dreams. There is a very special and subtle charm about her. The porcelain blossom cap quite naturally determined that 'Khadiya' shouldn't be wearing any clothes."

Himstedt invests her black dolls with the same attention to detail she devotes to her other projects. "All my dolls are equally special to me, no matter what ethnic background they reflect. I want my dolls to portray human life, and diversity is a very important part of it to me. Differences like the color of our skin are the characteristics that make us unique. Though the true beauty of a doll—like a person—comes from below the skin, it is the sum of its parts. And ultimately I hope that my dolls can contribute to a better understanding and appreciation of our diversity and individuality."

*Right: "Fatou," 26, vinyl; Opposite page: "Sveva,"*
*33 inches, vinyl*

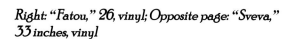

# DOUG JAMES & LAURA MEISNER

*"DLD has the power to create remarkably lifelike doll creations.*
*We are profoundly moved by their attentive expression and inner glow. They are*
*dynamic in form and style, communicating harmony of body and spirit."—BAW*

L ong-time friends and collaborators Doug James and Laura Meisner worked—together and separately—on numerous doll projects. They created the fashion dolls Willow & Daisy that debuted in 1999. (They came up with the original concept and designed both the body and all the fashions worn by the dolls for the first two years of their production.) The pair also designed a special limited line of Cissy dolls for Alexander Doll Company in 2001. A former conservationist of antique dolls for the Museum of the City of New York and an original member of The Ashton-Drake Galleries' Gene Team, Meisner designed many of the Gene doll's hairstyles as well as the outfits "Iced Coffee" and "Embassy Luncheon." James, also one of the original Gene Team designers, created more than eleven costumes for the Gene doll, including "Hello Hollywood," which won a Doll-of-the-Year (DOTY) award from *Doll Reader* magazine in 1998, and "Good-bye New York," which many consider to be the most popular Gene costume of all.

Outside the doll world, James has worked in the professional costume industry for more than twenty years, designing clothing and millinery for celebrities like Jack Nicholson, Rosie O'Donnell, Bette Midler and Jane Powell. His millinery work and costumes have appeared in numerous Broadway shows and motion pictures. In addition, he has taught costuming at Yale and Rutgers Universities, and is currently the assistant head of wardrobe for *Saturday Night Live* on NBC.

In 2002, the pair decided to team up on a project completely their own. The result was DLD International, through which they introduced their own fashion doll line called CED (a name based on the monograms of each of the dolls).

Sadly, in January of 2003, Meisner, struggling with depression and personal demons, took her own life, leaving James to carry on alone. Still shaken and struggling to re-organize in the wake of the tragedy, James nevertheless is determined to continue the company and the original vision and concept he shared with Meisner when they embarked on this joint venture.

Collectors themselves, James and Meisner set out to design their dream dolls. On their wish list: gorgeous fashions and the perfect body to show them off. Admiring the articulation of Dollikins and other similarly styled dolls, they nevertheless wanted to create a figure

*Above: "Constance Erin Dash," 19 inches, hard plastic;*
*Opposite page: "Colin Elia Dehan," 19 inches, hard*
*plastic*

70

whose proportions more closely resembled those of a real adult woman. The duo's initial three dolls were nineteen inches high and made of hard plastic with fourteen points of articulation for greater posing possibilities. The dolls' human-like proportions are in the elegant tradition of the Théâtre de la Mode mannequins.

Ethnic diversity was also a key design point for James and Meisner. While "Claire Elizabeth Daniels" was a blond American, the other two were "Cara Emile Duncan," a brunette with an Indonesian background, and "Constance Erin Dash," a brunette with a mixed Afro-Brazilian history. Following in the lovely tradition of her multicultural sisters, "Colin Elia Dehan" premiered later as the couple's first fully black doll.

"Laura and I have always been interested in different ethnicities. The vast majority of dolls available for collectors are either Caucasian or African American, so we wanted to point up that there are other peoples in the world, as well," says the Michigan-born James.

"We want to include everybody," the late Meisner, who was of Puerto Rican descent, once said.

The pair designed all the dolls and oversaw the sculpting process, which took place in China. For months they labored on the sculpt, working with an engineer to create a beautifully proportioned woman's figure, down to lovely, long finger-nailed hands that are even able to wear rings.

The dolls, limited to editions of 300, sell for about $350 each. James and Meisner opted not to give the dolls complicated story lines, preferring instead to concentrate on fabulous clothes. "This is a fashion doll created to celebrate fashion," James affirms. Accordingly, the dolls are dressed in fine silks, wools and laces. "Colin Elia Dehan," for instance, is a "Dark Angel" in a shapeless, white silk-chiffon dress with a burnout-velvet leaf pattern. The dressed doll also comes with crystal jewelry, silver evening sandals, thong panties and a parasol.

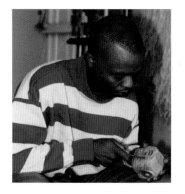

# KOR JANUARY

*"Kor allows the rich beauty of wood to transform old ideas into today's treasures. His dolls radiate creative beauty and soul. The uniqueness of his dolls emphasize the rare quality of this artist."* —BAW

*Above: "Kathy and Angela," 8½ inches and 7½ inches, maple and oak; Above left: "Sandy and Audrey," 14 inches, poplar wood*

You could say Kor January's artistic tendencies are in his blood. Born in Monrovia, Liberia, he grew up surrounded by creative influences. "My aunt Zena Holcombe made and sold dolls all her life. Seeing her example probably got me interested in making dolls myself," he says. "Every time I visited, her house was full of dolls. I remember when I was about eleven years old making some simple dolls of my own from clothes pegs. And I picked up painting from my brothers," adds January, one of eight children.

When it came time to decide on a profession, January, who has lived on and off in the United States and Liberia, naturally gravitated towards art. Saying he can't remember the last time he had a "real" job (he worked in the sewing department of a mascot costume-making factory for about six months and does part-time work cutting down trees), January confesses that "normal behavior, things and people don't attract me." For the past four years he's been pursuing the life of a full-time

artist. He's tried painting (everything from portraits to daycare-center murals), dollmaking and, most recently, welding metal sculptures. Dollmaking, however, remains his primary focus and livelihood. He's begun his own cottage industry. "I'll have about three people come in, one at a time, at various times throughout the year to help me with different aspects of the dollmaking process—the sanding, the staining, sewing, etc.—and I'll concentrate on carving the faces," he explains. "We'll make about fifty hands and fifty feet, and I'll have them on hand to make about thirty dolls a year. This way I can be working on several dolls at a time in various stages of completion."

*Above: "Valerie," 16 inches, wood;*
*Left: "Thelma," 16 inches, redwood*

Yet that's not to say his methods are in any way structured. January clearly leaves the goal setting and career planning to others. "I'm not big on the future. I take it day by day, doll by doll and moment to moment. I believe in enjoying each second to the maximum because the only thing I can count on is change. I like to experiment. Life is colorful, changing and it just is. I'm not about making statements—political, philosophical or of any kind. All I require of my art, myself or my life is that it is interesting and that it be enjoyed."

Not surprisingly, January's works—all one-of-a-kinds—are novel interpretations of reality; the world and its inhabitants as perceived through January's eyes and hands are a fanciful blend of fantasy and the surreal. "I deal with reality every day. With my art I escape into fantasy to create glimpses of dreams, visions of what I'd like life to be, or something that captures a moment or feeling in time that I want to re-create. I want my work to take you to a better place."

Perhaps because of their closer connection to the fanciful and imaginative, children are January's favorite subjects. "I'd say ninety percent of my work deals with children, and seventy-five percent with black subjects," he notes. "Creating dolls of children, especially their faces, challenges my ability, forcing me to be more focused and diverse in creating wood images. No two pieces are the same. Each piece allows me to explore and say something different."

Ranging in size from eight to sixteen inches, January's dolls are all made of different kinds of wood, and priced between $85 and $850.

January, who describes his style as "at times folkish, at times primitive," creates contemporary pieces with elements of the surreal. He strives to create dolls that convey a memory of a certain time. Although he admires all dollmakers, there is no one artist he seeks to emulate. "I'm not trying to be someone else's protegé or pattern myself after anyone. I admire all artists and see something special in at least one aspect of their work, and I take something from each one, but I am trying to carve my own path."

# ELIZABETH JENKINS

*"An expert in expressing vivacity, Elizabeth creates an explosion of movement and rhythm in her dolls. One can appreciate and enjoy the feeling of the magic and motion these dolls vibrate."—BAW*

A psychic told a young Elizabeth Jenkins that she'd become involved in a craft of "feminine origins" that had to do with "faces and color" and that she possessed a "unique ability to raise this to the highest art form." At the time, nothing seemed less likely. Jenkins, who had earned a degree in fine arts at the University of Missouri in her native Kansas City, and had also studied at Fashion Institute of Technology in New York City, was intent on her career as a theatrical costume designer. She quickly forgot about the prediction until twenty years later when—after having developed allergies to the chemicals she used in her work—she sat in a doctor's office and chanced upon a *DOLLS* magazine. "I was overwhelmed! Here was just the kind of project I had been dreaming of all my life—the chance to portray a character fully, with costume, hair and 'make-up,'" she says. "It truly felt like a date with destiny!"

*"Ma Rainey," 23 inches, LaDoll stoneclay*
*(Photo: Jim Hedstrom)*

The serendipitous elements continued with her first doll. "I had intended to make a little white girl wearing Christmas pajamas, and painting her toenails while waiting for Santa. As fate would have it, I fell asleep with the oven on, and the little girl came out dark purple. In a split second, I decided to fix the skin color by painting her brown. She turned out much more charming than the blonde I had planned. That was the first time I ever thought of making a black doll."

But it was far from the last. The following year, 1999, she "timidly" entered a local doll competition and won the grand prize for her "Kansas City Legend," while two of her other dolls earned Best of Category awards.

Encouraged, she decided to enter the Santa Fe Doll Art competition. While she traveled by plane to New Mexico, friends drove down with "Kansas City Legend," which became damaged during the long ride in the hot car. "My plane arrived late, and I only had minutes left to register for the competition, when I met my friends. I removed the doll from the box, saw that the cement holding the microphone in her hand had come loose, and quickly re-glued the part. However, some silver paint had popped off during the separation.

"We were wondering what to do when another couple from Kansas City miraculously showed up with a quick fix. They'd found a paint set—complete with brush and silver paint—that someone had left behind in their motel room. In seconds, the paint was re-touched and the doll registered. To the delight of our Kansas City 'team,' she won the Robert McKinley Award for best new talent!"

With such signs pointing the way, Jenkins couldn't help but continue to follow the path of dollmaking. Although she makes some fantasy creatures and portraits, to date, about fifty percent of Jenkins' pieces are black dolls.

Her dolls, priced from $500 to $2,000, have been predominantly one-of-a-kinds, but she hopes to start making five-piece editions in stone clay.

For her first black dolls, Jenkins surreptitiously studied black acquaintances and strangers. "I began to compare hand pigmentation, skull shape, body types and facial features in a new way," she says. "I had usually looked at blacks—at everyone—searching for the similarities that unite us as humans. Now I was focusing on the

*Above: "Dancerman," 23 inches, LaDoll stoneclay;*
*Left: "Bessie Smith," 23 inches, LaDoll stoneclay*
*(Photos: Jim Hedstrom)*

differences. It was nerve-wracking at first. Imagine me—a blond, middle-aged, middle-class mid-westerner—staring voraciously at strangers of another ethnic group. In the end, though, I discovered that most people prefer to be looked over rather than overlooked."

Dollmaking opened Jenkins up to new levels of human perception and artistic expression. "We want to see the artist's hand in a work of art," Jenkins explains. "We also want it open to a small amount of interpretation, so that viewers have to project something of their own imaginations onto the work. This investment of emotion is what makes the audience a participant in the process of creative dialogue. By not supplying all the information, you make your audience reach out and take the art into their hearts. Doll figures, like jazz, are intended deliberately to be an intimate emotional experience for the audience."

Jenkins' dolls have been embraced with overwhelming enthusiasm. "I began to see what a shortage of appealing black images were out there, especially in the doll world, where blacks were often portrayed as humorous caricatures or bland, white-washed fashion dollies," she notes. "I believe that dignity and glamour, and the beauty that is truth can be shown in black figures today. What I've seen through my collectors is that the notion of physical attractiveness is expanding to include many facial forms and colors.

"I have always found that creating a portrait of someone lets you stand in his or her shoes like nothing else," she continues. "Through deeply contemplating the placement of lines in a face and finding out the story of the person's life, you almost get to be the other person for a moment. For me, creating my doll characters is the same thing actors do when they 'put on' other personalities. From my historical research and from making portraits of black musicians, the horizons of my understanding of 'the black experience' have radically expanded."

Empathy is the essential emotion Jenkins strives to evoke with her three-dimensional portraits. "I want viewers of my dolls to feel they are meeting the gaze of a real being, captured in one moment of existence. I want them to say, 'I know that person!' which is one step away from saying, 'I see me in that person.'"

*Top: "Kansas City Legend," 18 inches, LaDoll stoneclay; Right: "Ya Better Believe It!" 23 inches, LaDoll stoneclay (Photos: Jim Hedstrom)*

# HELEN KISH

*"Enchanting, encompassing and ethereal are among the adjectives I find myself using when describing Helen Kish's dolls. She uses her artistic intuition and talents to create memorable dolls with innocent faces and alluring charm. She compels us to see the world through a child's eye."—BAW*

Like any "good" little girl, Helen Kish would religiously attend Mass every Sunday with her parents and seven siblings. But possessed of an imaginative, dreamy nature and hands that preferred to be fashioning her own paper doll designs, Kish confesses that she sometimes had a difficult time following the service and retreated into artistic contemplation instead.

"I couldn't understand Latin, but I could silently study the statuary," says the artist in relating her life-long passion for the figurative arts. "My affinity was for the faces and the hands of the figures. Weekends spent with my cousins afforded me the opportunity to study yet another sculptor's interpretation of sacred subjects in a different church. Although I was too young to see the parallels at the time, I've studied dolls in the same way. My cousins Katie and Billie had a closet full of Nancy Ann Story Book dolls from the 1940s and 1950s. I'm sure that they all thought little Helen was a bit dotty as

**"Willy," 12½ inches, vinyl**

she stood in front of that case for hours staring at those little beauties."

No one thinks her foolish or unfocused these days. After studying at the University of Colorado and the Rocky Mountain School of Art, the Denver native—who makes the city her home base of operations for Kish & Company, the doll business she established in 1990 with her husband, Tamas—went about building a stellar doll-making career that spans nearly three decades. A member of the National Institute of American Doll Artists (NIADA) since 1980, Kish has won numerous awards and distinctions, and has had her work exhibited in museums such as the Rosalie Whyel Museum of Doll Art in Bellevue, Washington, and the Musée des Arts Décoratifs in Paris, France.

Preferring to sculpt in stoneware ("I love the texture and immediacy"), she currently designs anywhere from six to twenty-four dolls a year. Kish's one-of-a-kind pieces, usually in stoneware and fiber, sell for $2,500 to $12,000 each; her limited-edition porcelains (issued in five- to thirty-piece editions) cost between $350 and $1,500; and her vinyl pieces (75- to 950-piece editions) range from $199 to $950. She's made dolls as small as three inches and as large as fifty-four inches, but most fall within the eight-inch to twenty-four-inch range. Also currently available are Kish's "The Girls of Many Lands" series, which was launched in September of 2002 by the Pleasant Company.

Nearly a third of her one-of-a-kind figures have been black or African. The majority of Kish's other dolls of color have portrayed black children or adults, with just a few Hispanics or Asians. (Kish is currently embarking on a new project to design pieces depicting Native Americans.)

A child of the turbulent 1960s, she felt the weighty impact of the Civil Rights Movement, and was at first hesitant to approach black subjects. "I am most conscious of portraying my black subjects with utmost dignity," she stresses. "Early on, I was concerned to the point of being fearful of even attempting to sculpt a black child. Back in the 1980s, I sent a photograph of one of my early black dolls to a fellow NIADA member, Roberta Bell, for her critique. Her kind words encouraged me to continue. And so I have.

"What draws me to certain black characters is no different than what draws me to any other character—the beauty of the forms, the intensity of the feeling in a face, an infectious smile," says Kish. "I also love the variety of colors, textures of hair and skin that are so unique to the African peoples. Then, there is the unique sense of style and color that Africans and African Americans bring to their dress. And the ornamentation!

"As with anything I do, it's the sculpting that I most enjoy," Kish continues. "It's always a challenge to get the

bones right, to animate the face and then to paint life into the eyes!

"When I was sculpting and painting 'Sweet Home Chicago,' I couldn't get over how much he reminded me of one of my brothers—Michael. But then, there was an actor (the black actor Demond Wilson) who played the son on the television show *Sandford and Son* who was my brother Mike 'in living color.' They had the same mannerisms, the same gait. It just goes to show you that we really are all family."

Indeed, when regarded in overview, the entire body of Kish's work—while diverse in mediums, subject matter, race, age and sex—undeniably shares a certain commonality. "I have developed an identity of design. People do recognize my work as my work even where it is not credited. What I hear collectors say is that they recognize the sculpting of the lips, the painting of the eyes, the hands," notes the artist, who describes her style as a type of "idealized realism."

# SUSAN KREY

*"Beguiling with feelings, Susan's indescribable dolls help you to experience the wonders of doll artistry by reconnecting you with your childhood dreams. With simplistic beauty, they travel on a timeless journey into your very heart."—BAW*

Born in London, England, on July 29, 1943, Susan Krey earned a Royal Society of Arts degree from Hornsey College of Art in London. After graduation, she joined her mother and sister in Australia, where she found jobs as a fabric designer and as an art teacher. After meeting and marrying American-born Tim Krey, she moved to the United States, where the couple went about starting and raising a family.

Apart from her children's playthings, Krey wasn't particularly aware of dolls until one fateful day in 1980 when her husband bought a doll magazine for her. "I couldn't put it down," remembers Krey. "It literally fell apart. It was natural for me to want to make dolls, as I had a degree from a leading London art school where, among other subjects, I had studied painting, fabric design and sculpture. It was the perfect combination!"

By 1981, knowing she'd finally found her heart's career, Krey was happily making and selling her own dolls. "I already painted pictures, but my love for babies—I had five of my own—and little children made dollmaking a natural outlet for me. I could just keep making babies, which eventually helped me put all my real Krey babies through school." In fact, her business—Krey Baby Doll Company—did so well that, by 1991, her husband had quit his job to help her run it. With the exception of a brief time in 1993, when she designed a few pieces for The Ashton-Drake Galleries, Krey has concentrated on the "family" enterprise.

Krey creates one-of-a-kind pieces as well as limited editions (with edition sizes between just twelve and twenty-five pieces). Prices for her dolls range from $2,000 to $4,000; their sizes vary from twenty-six to thirty-two inches. She's worked in clay, porcelain, wax-over-porcelain and wax, but her favorite is wax-over-porcelain. With this combination, Krey explains, "You can get a beautiful finish and the dolls are life-like. It adds a translucent look to the skin on many dolls."

She currently designs five to ten dolls a year. Almost every year the artist creates at least one ethnic doll for her collection. "I love black dolls and Asian dolls, but my favorites are mulattos," she notes. For her, the appeal of creating black dolls lies in the variety of hues. "I love the sultry color of ethnic subjects. From black to creamy brownish yellows with black, brown, green, gray and even blue eyes, the combinations are so unusual

and striking," she states.

"I like to create black dolls because they're an unusual contrast to my other dolls," Krey elaborates. "I love working with color, so having a range of skin color is important to me." On the down side, she says, "It is more expensive and time-consuming to produce dark-colored bisque because the heavy pigment of the slip has a tendency to separate and cause streaking when fired. I often have to put a wash over the whole face to achieve the right hue, which can be tricky."

Although she insists she doesn't approach creating her black dolls any differently than any of her others, Krey does admit to holding them a little in awe. "Perhaps I do regard them with a little more reverence. Not being black myself and having been raised in England where I rarely saw black people, I guess I'm just fascinated by them."

"Ebony," a 1920s flapper girl bride, was inspired by a Lladró figure. "The turn of her head and her gentle face, the warmth of her skin against her veil create a striking contrast, yet the effect is soft, making this doll a sellout among collectors," says Krey. When people look at her dolls—no matter their race or shade—Krey hopes "the observer will feel something besides 'she's pretty.' I want to evoke a feeling, perhaps a remembering, of something good that touches the heart."

*Opposite page: "Ebony," 32 inches, porcelain*

# LISA LICHTENFELS

*"If creativity is the gift of gods, Lisa has been chosen. Her dolls are messengers of truth and beauty. Masterfully 'sculpted' of fabric, so remarkable in realism, they elicit our awe and wonder."—BAW*

Regarded by many as the doll artist's artist, Lisa Lichtenfels inspires admiration and controversy with her striking and often sensual works that celebrate the human body with superb anatomical and soulful accuracy. In the foreword of *Figures in Fabric* (Portfolio Press, 2001), the late John Darcy Noble, a past curator of the Toy Collection at the Museum of the City of New York and former *DOLLS* magazine columnist, wrote: "...this is true of all of Lisa's figures. In some magical way they are, none of them, just descriptions or depictions, but living presences, with—I would swear—hearts and minds of their own...I can find no other word with which to describe Lisa's amazing techniques; they are truly awesome."

As with all her pieces, Lichtenfels' portrayals of black characters leave viewers shaking their heads in wonder at her x-ray vision clarity into her characters' souls. This quest to portray the inner psyche through a doll was imprinted into Lichtenfels' consciousness during her early formative years. "I saw my first doll when I was four or five years old," says the artist, who was born in 1958 in Erie, Pennsylvania. "I was at an auction and wandered away from the sale items of a bankrupt German Pennsylvania farm. In the back room, I saw an elderly farmer with a puppen. It was a portrait of his daughter as she looked before she died. It was housed in a box with personal items and charms to lure her soul. It was a spell cast by her father so he would not be without her. Puppen is

loosely translated to English as 'doll,' but it has many more shades of meaning. The ancient root word is 'pupe,' which means 'the image you see of yourself when you look someone else in the eye.' The dark center part of the eye where it can be seen is called the pupil, as in the student who 'lives in the eye of the teacher.' A puppet is a puppen that moves. So I became very interested in puppen as ghost catchers, as forms of character and magical objects."

For twenty-three years she's conjured her own brand of magic to capture the lovely ghosts of her imagination and bring them into the world of the living. Although she's worked in oil paint, illustration, line and three-dimensional animation, Lichtenfels prefers to express herself through soft sculptures because, for her, they are the most like skin. "Conventional forms of art bore me," she confesses. "As an artist, I am attracted to dolls. I don't know the reasons why exactly; it is just perfect for me."

After graduating from the Pennsylvania Governor's School for the Arts, Lichtenfels attended the Philadelphia College of Art where she majored in illustration and filmmaking. Upon graduation, she moved to California and worked as an apprentice animator at the Disney Studios in Burbank. She began selling her dolls in 1981 and by 1985 had captivated the doll world, earning entry into the prestigious

*Left: "Astar," 38 inches, mixed media soft sculpture; Opposite page: "Masai Warrior," 29 inches, mixed media soft sculpture*

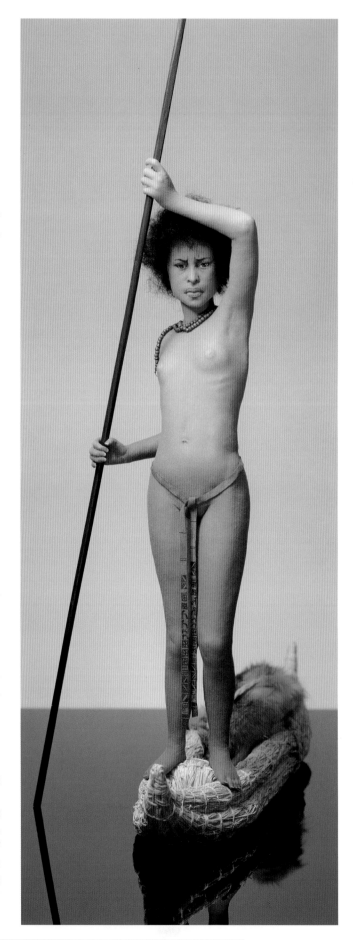

National Institute of American Doll Artists (NIADA). Other honors and awards include several Massachusetts Cultural Resources Project Grants (the artist currently lives and works in Springfield, Massachusetts); a three-year appointment (from 1986 to 1989) as Artist in Residence for the Massachusetts Cultural Education Collaborative; and an Artist Fellowship Grant from the Springfield Cultural Council and the Massachusetts Cultural Council. In addition to making an instructional video that was released in 1999 by Rockfish, she has written two books, *The Basic Body, Soft Sculpture Techniques of Lisa Lichtenfels* (Carruth Press, 1995) and the aforementioned *Figures in Fabric*.

Each year the artist creates up to six one-of-a-kind pieces. They range in size from five inches to five feet, but are typically less than thirty inches. "Each doll has its own world of emotion. I would hope a viewer would connect to the personality or the soul within," says Lichtenfels, noting she is often drawn to black characters because living in a neighborhood where three-quarters of her neighbors are African American, she is surrounded by marvelous inspiration.

"Astar," the ancient African incarnation of Aphrodite, is pure transcendent elegance in her proud, elemental beauty that needs no worldly enhancements. The beauty in "Zora" springs not so much from the figure's outer form as from her inner radiance. With this portrait of the Harlem Renaissance writer Zora Neale Hurston, Lichtenfels sought to convey the "humor, intelligence and boundless youthful vigor I had found in her writing. The exuberance of her person seemed like a great spiritual freedom."

Eye-fooling anatomical realism is a salient element of all of Lichtenfels' work. One has only to look at figures like "Masai Warrior," a paean celebration of the beauty of the male form in all its masculine athleticism, or "Motu Girl," with its body-mimicking articulation of the waist and hips, to appreciate and stand in awe of Lichtenfels' mastery of her chosen medium.

# CHRIS MALONE

*"Originality, intriguing, modernistic, and sometimes futuristic in style, Malone's dolls open the door to an incredible journey of creativity and art in the world of dolls that challenges our imagination. His dolls are powerful and unforgettable."—BAW*

**"I** have always been into dolls," declares Chris Malone, a Washington, DC-based artist who has been making dolls professionally for the past twelve years. "When I was growing up, being a little boy, I was given trucks and footballs—'boys' things—and my sisters were given dolls. But I would play with my toys and my sisters' dolls," he relates of his childhood memories as the middle child in a family of five kids. "My parents thought I would 'grow out' of the doll thing. I guess I didn't!"

As a boy, Malone surprised everyone—including himself—by creating the head of a horse from clay for a 4-H project, which won a blue ribbon. Of his unusual career choices, Malone explains, "I have always been artistic and drawn to the unusual, so I feel that I was predestined to do what I do now."

After leaving his family's fifty-acre farm in Indiana, this Midwest boy joined the Navy in search of adventure. Two years later, his quest for seeking the "wild" life led him to taking jobs such as an exotic-bird keeper at the Franklin Park Zoo in Boston, Massachusetts, a high-priced fashion model, and most recently, a zookeeper at the Smithsonian Institution's National Zoo in Washington, DC.

*Right: "Holler," 21 inches, Cernit;*
*Opposite page: "Taking a Break,"*
*20 inches, Cernit*

Somewhere along this life trajectory, he unexpectedly discovered his true calling in a Tiffany's display window. Like a kid with his nose pressed to the pane, he took in the fabulous clay pieces of a well-known doll artist, and whammo—instant connection!

"I figured with my artistic background I could learn to sculpt dolls myself, and I went out and bought clay," relates the self-taught artist of this pivotal juncture. It wasn't long before he was creating and selling his imaginative pieces.

"Creating dolls allows me to recall certain feelings and emotions derived from people I have met and places I have visited, and to express them in clay. My work is original and often tends to be controversial and thought-provoking," he notes. "The dolls' facial expressions trigger more than 'oh, isn't it cute.'

"My dolls show the range of emotions. Many of them are black. When I first started, there were very few whimsical dolls of color, and I wanted people of color to see themselves depicted in this art form and have fun with dolls, too. My dolls also make political statements. After all, anyone who lives in Washington, DC, is bound to have a political opinion—on everything!"

When asked to describe his artistic style and what sets him and his work apart, Malone responds: "My work is truly contemporary and original with an exaggerated design element. I am not looking to please any one person or specific market. I only make what is inside of me. My dolls are what they are.

"You make what you know," Malone continues. "Many times I have come across a black doll design and it did not seem to go far enough in expressing any genuine emotion or character or thought, perhaps out of fear by the artist of going too far or not far enough. Being a black artist, I feel it is my duty to probe as deep as possible to find true feeling and emotion in my black dolls."

Malone, who has been featured in publications such as *DOLLS* magazine, the *Washington Post* and the *Boston Globe*, creates only one-of-a-kind dolls; they are priced between $45 and $2,000, and can vary in size from about four to twenty-three inches. Although he's also tried Super Sculpey, Sculpey and Fimo, Malone works mainly in Cernit and often uses feathers collected from his father's farm.

"I really love looking at a ball of clay and being able to see what is inside of it before I start to make it. Creating dolls has been a source of comfort and joy to me, and I only hope that my dolls can make others feel the same way," says Malone, who designs and sculpts about twenty-seven dolls each year.

Projecting what new paths he might embark upon, Malone says, "I am very open to my future as a doll artist. When you are an adult, you are supposed to put away your fantasy world. I never have. I hope to give out good, and in turn, have good things come to me."

# DORIS McGILLAN

*"Skillfully, Doris produces extraordinary dolls in vibrant African textiles and cloth. Cultural heritage is important to her and is reflected in her dolls. Each doll is an heirloom to be passed down from one generation to the next."—BAW*

Dolls weren't in Doris E. McGillan's original game plan. She began her professional career as an international representative for Chemical Workers AFL/CIO, traveling extensively as part of her labor-union negotiations. Along the way, she discovered one of her many passions—missionary work. As a missionary for the Progressive National Baptist Convention, she traveled to The Congo, Kenya, Ghana, Senegal, Haiti, the Middle East and South America.

It was her charitable pursuits that brought her latent dollmaking talents to light. Back in 1991, she was faced with the task of coming up with a craft project for her church's art show. "I wanted to make something by hand from scratch. The only problem was that I didn't have any talent," she recalls with a laugh and a shake of the head. After thinking long and hard—not to mention being turned down repeatedly after asking to team up on others'

craft projects—she was given a suggestion by her daughter: Why not create African dolls small enough to fit into glass display cases? Why not indeed, thought McGillan, who went about doing just that, drawing heavily from her already extensive knowledge of and familiarity with the clothing, designs and colors of numerous African nationalities. "I wear a lot of African clothes myself, so it was fairly easy to design my dolls after my own clothing," McGillan notes.

The eight dolls McGillan made for the church's art show all sold, and they set in motion a domino effect of sales and word of mouth that would eventually lead her to start her own home-based company, Heritage Designs. In the process, her dolls have found homes in museums, design studios, galleries and gift shops around the globe, and with celebrities like Anita Baker and Senator Hillary Rodham Clinton. In 1995, McGillan

*Below: "Cotton Picker," 13 inches, wild grass, wire and wooden ball;*
*Inset: "Market Place," 13 inches, wild grass, wire and wooden ball;*
*Opposite page: "Jubilee," 13 inches, wild grass, wire and wooden ball*

was inducted into the Leo Moss Black Doll Hall of Fame in Philadelphia. A juried member of the Pennsylvania Guild of Craftsmen, she was the featured artist (in 2001) at The Hickman of West Chester, Pennsylvania.

She prides herself on creating meticulously researched ethnic dolls that are affordably priced (they sell from about $65 to $120). Her Bamboo Collection represents people living along the Indian Ocean in Kenya, Lamu and Mombassa. The Marketplace Collection re-creates African and Caribbean market-places, which McGillan describes as a "kaleidoscope of color and excitement." The Quilter Doll series pays homage to Harriet Tubman, the Quakers and abolitionists who created the Underground Railroad, while The Cotton Picker series is dedicated to the mothers and fathers who fought valiantly to keep their children with them during a dark period when tearing families apart was as commonplace as dividing bales of cotton for the market. Other dolls include the Royal Collection, the Mudcloth Collection and the Yesterday Collection.

McGillan's craft has become a way to get in touch with her roots and convey her love and knowledge of African culture to others. "The African designs, vibrant colors and rich, textured fabrics speak to my soul, which inspires me to create and express my knowledge through my art," she says. One only has to look at a piece like "The African Dancer" to get swept up in the artist's celebration of the African beat, rhythm and body movement as suggested by McGillan's artful posing of the doll's body. "To experience the African dance inspired and compelled me to capture this electrifying art form. It penetrates one's very soul," says McGillan.

In addition to running Heritage Designs, McGillan continues her mission work and lecturing on the history behind her dolls. Making an impact on young minds is especially gratifying, and she's found that she gets as much as she gives in such exchanges. For instance, "The Cotton Picker" was born out of a discussion with a second-grade student who said that she would rather learn about her own history than of the more distant and, to her, alien African culture. "This gave birth to my collection entitled African/American Trailblazers," explains McGillan. "This has been my most rewarding and sought-after collection. It gives significant insight about the character, which represents a defined culture and heritage."

As in the way she lives her life, McGillan's dolls exemplify this caring woman's personal motto of "I just want to serve."

*"African Dancer," 13 inches, wild grass, wire and wooden ball*

# PAULINE MIDDLETON

*"A vision for the future, Pauline's gorgeous dolls provide us with a rare chance to embrace every aspect of our humanity. We are awed by all the dolls that she has created."—BAW*

Out of personal grief Pauline Middleton has found joy in creating her spiritual children in porcelain. In 1976, she suffered the loss of twin girls who were stillborn. "In the difficult and emotional times that followed, I took a hobby class in reproduction dollmaking. It was part of the healing process for me. It was so wonderful to re-create a beautiful little child. It was during that course, and after working with those beautiful little faces, that I was overcome with the feeling that I could sculpt faces like that. So, after taking a lump of clay, and working on it for nine months or so, a sleeping baby was created. I then read as many books as I could on mold making and dollmaking, and have been learning ever since. It has become my life!"

A hairdresser by trade, the Aussie native had no formal art training. "My style is my own," says Middleton, who has been seriously making dolls for about two decades. "My aim is always to sculpt and produce a very life-like doll. I strive for the perfect likeness. I think that a feature of my work is the skin tone I achieve. The dolls are poured in white porcelain; I mix a few colors of china paint together, and then do light washes with a firing each time. There can be five to six paint firings before I get the lovely skin tone that I am striving for. I have not had any formal training, therefore have not had anyone's ideas influence my work." Middleton adds.

That's not to say she does not have doll artists she admires. Indeed, she's vocal in her admiration of people like Hildegard Günzel, Lorna Miller Sands, Wiltrud Stein, Ella Hass, Anne Mitrani and fellow Aussies, Steve and Angela Clark. She's also quick to share credit for her

*"Emma," 25 inches, porcelain*

own dolls, which she's been making full-time for the last eight years with her business and personal life partner, Bob Brown. "Bob makes the molds and does a lot of the pouring," says Middleton. "We work together to clean the porcelain, and I do the painting and all the finishing. Our endeavor is to create the most life-like children we can. We keep striving to improve. We have worked hard to gather around us some of the world's best crafts people to help with our creations. We have friends now who work with us to provide great wigs (thanks, Dulcie), beautifully smocked and embroidered clothes (thanks, Debbie and Nolene), wonderful eyes (thanks, Greg), and lovely hand-made leather shoes (thanks, Joyce). We could not be presenting the dolls that we do without their wonderful skills."

Radiating the innocence and vulnerability of youth, Middleton's charmingly realistic dolls, ninety-five percent of which are black, often inspire intense reactions. Middleton recounts an amusing incident that occurred several years ago after a doll show during a hot Melbourne summer. "A lady observed me from a distance as I placed one of my 'girls' into the back seat and fastened the seat belt and locked the car," Middleton relates. "As I walked away, she came running over and was so abusive and disgusted that I had left a child in the car with no windows open on such a hot day! She was most embarrassed when told it was a doll. I guessed that by then the dolls were becoming pretty lifelike!"

To create her dolls' amazingly human qualities, Middleton works from photographs, searching through magazines and photography books for inspirational shots. Middleton and Brown, who have eight grandchildren

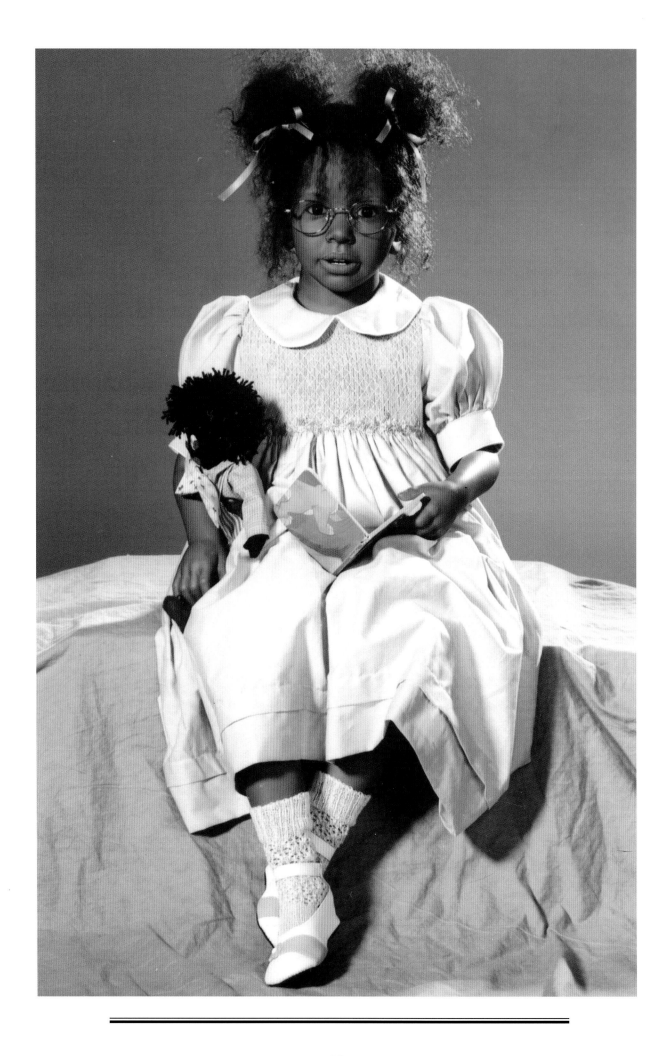

between them, also love to study their expressions and poses. "Finding just the right expression or action that I want to sculpt can be a long and difficult task," she admits, "but once I find the right picture, I cannot wait to get at the clay! It is not just the faces that I look for. I sculpt new hands and feet for each doll, and so the poses of the hands and feet are equally important. I put a lot of thought into how the dolls will interact with each other when they are shown together."

Although she'll occasionally create one-of-a-kind pieces, Middleton primarily makes three to four dolls in limited editions of twenty. The dolls, typically twelve to thirty-three inches high, sell for $2,400 to $2,600. She likes to work with earthenware clay for the sculpting and porcelain for the doll.

"My art is very important to me," Middleton notes. "My special afternoons are spent sitting outside in the shade and sculpting a new little person. I can be lost in their magic for many, many hours.

"I just love the features of black children—the gorgeous skin tone, their fuller lips, broad nose and oh, those beautiful, big eyes! Over the years I sculpted a lot of Australian aboriginal children, and now find that I do a combination of our indigenous Australians and African-American children. The enjoyment really comes when someone chooses my work and you can tell that they just love it.

"Some people love the work purely as a work of art—a realistic sculpture that they can display in their house. Others bond to the doll and just love to hold it as if it were a child. We once had a lovely older lady buy a doll on layaway. She paid over many months and we arranged for her to pick up her doll at a show we were attending. When I passed the baby doll to her, she gently cuddled it to her breast. I looked at her face to see the tears streaming down her cheeks as she looked into the doll's eyes. That is why I work! There can be no bigger thrill for an artist than to evoke such emotion."

# LINDA MURRAY

*'Linda's unprecedented fervor to create wonderful, high-quality dolls has left an indelible impression on the world, reflecting unsurpassed doll artistry. It is exciting to watch her add porcelain pieces to her unique ShellCloth designs."—BAW*

Despite not having any formal doll training, London-born Linda Murray has been making beautiful dolls for more than twenty-five years. After turning a cherished hobby—begun when she made her first doll at the age of eleven—into a full-time doll-making enterprise, Murray has raked in the honors. She now boasts more than twenty major international awards for her work.

"I've always been passionate about dolls, right from birth! My mom hated them, and my twin sister, Helen, and I never had any. Hence, a life-long passion—shared by Helen—for acquiring and making dolls," says Murray.

The majority of Murray's dolls have been made using a unique hard-formed translucent cloth, which the artist invented and has trademarked as ShellCloth, a system that requires twelve coatings of various solutions to achieve the dolls' life-like appearances. That may change, though, as she's recently discovered the benefits of porcelain. "Up to now ShellCloth has been my favorite medium as it is entirely my own and gives a very individual look to the dolls that cannot be successfully re-created in any other medium," she says. "Just lately, though, I have been experimenting in porcelain, and I really love the perfection it brings; a perfection completely impossible in ShellCloth, where it is incredibly challenging and time-consuming to achieve skin tones, especially black skin tones!"

Murray currently sculpts about ten to twenty new heads each year. "I have been working in editions of twenty, sometimes ten in ShellCloth," she notes. "I hope to do more one-of-a-kind and more limited editions of maybe five in both porcelain and ShellCloth." Her dolls sell for between $1,000 and $3,000, and are about twenty to thirty-six inches high.

Crafted with great thought and love, all of Murray's creations—whether beguiling small boys and girls, appealing toddlers or elegant ladies—are unique. Only one mold is ever made from any sculpture so that production numbers are severely limited. Although issued in small limited editions, all of the dolls are technically and artistically one-of-a-kind pieces, as each has individually hand-painted faces and limbs.

A significant amount of Murray's work is devoted to multicultural dolls. "I love ethnic subjects—the different bone structures and facial details make sculpting so much more exciting. From black dolls to Oriental, from Eurasian to Hispanic, I try to do them all," the artist says.

"Black is definitely beautiful," says Murray, who notes she bases many of her black dolls on magazine photographs. "Whether it be in a child, a baby or an adult, a depth of character seems easier to achieve with a black doll. They 'speak' to me. I find them the most

*Left: "Ali" and "Aisha," 26 and 28 inches, both of ShellCloth and cloth; Opposite page: "Moesha," 32 inches, porcelain*

stunning of all dolls when realism is perfected in both sculpting and skin tone. There is a natural magnificence, and although for me, this realism is harder to achieve, the end result makes black dolls the most rewarding of all to create."

"Ali" and "Aisha," both from Murray's 2002 Angels in Boots series, and "Thabo" and "Tanzi," from the artist's Golden Days Collection of 2001, are typical examples of the artist's ShellCloth pieces. Released in 2003, "Moesha" is Murray's first porcelain piece and, she says, "I have to admit to it being my favorite!"

*"Thabo" and "Tanzi," 25 and 28 inches, both of ShellCloth and cloth*

# ANNE MYATT

*"Anne is an exceptionally talented doll artist who is able to project a serene, inner happiness that gives vitality to her dolls. Uniquely costumed, each of her creations, representing ancestral lines, is not only a realistic adventure but a magnificent learning odyssey."—BAW*

**66** I remember making dolls at the early age of nine or ten," reminisces Anne Myatt, speaking of her childhood in Jackson, Mississippi. "As children, my sister and I believed our dolls came to life at midnight, and we would try to stay awake to catch them, but we never did. I made dolls out of whatever I could—out of bottles with corn silk hair and out of sticks with hair of curled rope.

"I never threw a doll away. I loved my dolls even after their heads had fallen off. Once I found an old doll in the snow and brought it home and dried it out. This old worn-out doll became one of my favorites. Some of my dolls bring back fond memories. I can remember feisty little Vicky, a rag doll who could face up to any situation; lovable little Donnie; Buster the clown, who could always draw a smile; Royal Lady; and Mandy, the last doll I received for Christmas when I was sixteen. I had her until I went away to nursing school. I lost Mandy in a flood, and it was as if I had lost a member of my family."

These days Myatt manages to work her "family" of dolls in between her demanding work schedule as a registered nurse. Designing and making about seven to ten dolls a year, Myatt began selling her one-of-a-kind creations twelve years ago under the company name of Like Me Dolls. She works mostly in cloth, noting, "I like its warm, organic feel. It lets me take my time and forgives my mistakes."

Myatt calculates that about ninety-five percent of all her work represents black individuals. "I think you create best what you know best," she explains. "My dolls are based on realism. I guess my knowledge of anatomy leads me to strive for reality in the doll form."

Given her penchant for realism, accurately capturing depth of feeling in the facial expressions and representing the diversity and nuances of black skin tones are key features of Myatt's work. Consequently, she finds sculpting faces to be the most satisfying and challenging part of the dollmaking process. "I enjoy coming up with a new and different creation with each doll. I love getting emotion to show," Myatt says of her pieces, which range in price from $500 to $1,500, and are about ten to twenty inches high.

"It is very important to show that we come in different colors. Because I work in cotton knit, I often have to dye the fabric to come up with the right shade. I have recently started adding the lighter color to the palms and

*"To Market," 17 inches, 6 inches, Super Sculpey covered with knit*

soles of the feet," says the artist whose dolls run the gamut from dark brown to lighter-skinned African-American complexions.

Myatt is especially partial to portraying mothers and children together, and creating a flow of feeling between the dolls and the viewers. With "Sweet Dreams," for instance, she has rendered a loving moment between mother and child that draws the viewer into the warm intimacy of a shared embrace. With "Hagar and Ishmael"—which earned an Award of Excellence nomination in 2001 from *DOLLS* magazine—the artist sought to convey outrage and determination. "When I made this doll, I saw such anger in her eyes," the artist relates. "I knew she wanted to share the story of the wronged Egyptian slave and her child saved from the desert."

"To Market" portrays a busy mother and her baby, whose face is beaming with an infectious grin. "I love to see babies doing something unexpected when their mothers cannot see their faces. Often strangers are smiling and communicating with the infant while the mother goes on about her business," Myatt explains.

Myatt is humbly grateful for the satisfaction and rewards dolls have brought into her life. "I feel blessed that God has given me this talent," she declares. "I try to pray before I begin each doll and ask that He will take my hands and let my work be for His glory. I know that all I do comes only from Him."

*Above: "Queen of Sheba," 20 inches, Super Sculpey covered with knit; Opposite page, top: "Sweet Dreams," 19 inches, 9 inches, Super Sculpey covered with knit; Bottom left: "Hagar and Ishmael," 20 inches, 9 inches, Super Sculpey covered with knit; Bottom right: "Litt'l Red," 20 inches, Super Sculpey covered with knit*

# SHIRLEY NIGRO~HILL

*"We are fortunate to witness these marvelous doll creations. Shirley's legendary dolls stimulate the life force which lives within us, and communicate a reality that makes us alive with doll magic and wonder."—BAW*

A self-described "dollmaking junkie," Shirley Nigro-Hill has been crafting and selling her dolls since she was about ten years old. "My mom gave me a magazine to look at in the doctor's office one time and it had an article on dolls made from socks and old clothing with embroidered faces, and that was it," she relates. "Armed with my brother's new socks, some clothing I didn't care for, and a little thread and yarn, I went to work and have been feeding my 'habit' ever since."

Nigro-Hill, who studied fine arts, model making and drafting at New York's Genesee Community College, goes on to relate, "I paint, draw and sculpt, but I don't think I chose dolls or even had a choice. I believe it was imprinted in my psyche, much like what happens to ducklings after hatching, following the first thing they see, thinking it's their mom. Well, with me being the first girl in the family after three boys and the first granddaughter, I just know someone held some kind of doll over me while cooing baby talk at me. So you see, I never had a chance!"

Working primarily with cloth and paperclay, Nigro-Hill makes homey and huggable pieces from her home base in Batavia, New York, where she was born and still resides. "I feel that, just like real people, all of my dolls are one-of-a-kind and special," she notes. "It's hard for me to say how much of my work is devoted to ethnic subjects because my dolls develop into their own personalities. But I'd venture that about seventy-five percent of my dolls wind up deciding to be black, Hispanic, Oriental, Native American or multicultural. I do people, and we do come in all shapes, sizes and colors. I just love doing personalities who are warm, giving and have a story to tell."

Nigro-Hill's dolls vary in price from $45 to $900, and measure from four to twenty-four inches in height. Many of the dolls' faces are formed by applying paperclay, felt or some other type of cloth to a plastic mask (made by heating plastic and forming it over a sculpted face), then hand-painting the features. She fashions the clothing using old fabrics. "I like to combine the old with the new to give the feeling that our past is just as important as our future," Nigro-Hill explains. "My work should give us pride in knowing where we have come from and the comfort to see us through whatever comes our way. I want my dolls to say that and to feel like an old friend. As you look at my dolls you will see a reflection of my life and of the people around me."

Nigro-Hill hopes her dolls rekindle the feeling of a "childhood memory, someone dear, something that brings comfort, a smile, maybe a laugh." With "Special Day," for instance, Nigro-Hill—inspired by her own daughters' enthusiasm—tried to capture a little girl's anticipation of all the wonderful things that might be waiting for her on a special day, perhaps a birthday, an outing with a family member or a big event at school. In "Sunday Best" she strove to evoke the "girly" feeling of putting on a pretty dress and getting all dolled up. In short, Nigro-Hill seeks to portray life at its most basic, and at its best.

*Below: "Special Day," 13 inches, paperclay and cloth; Opposite page: "Sunday Best," 9 inches, cloth over artist's plastic mask*

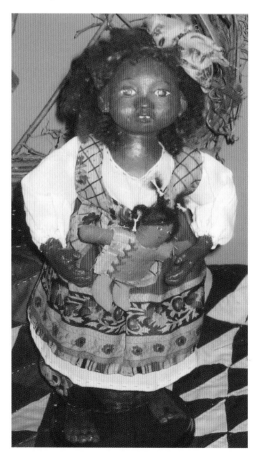

# Mel Odom & Michael Evert

*"Magnificent! All the right elements of styles and superb costuming are united in Mel and Michael's strikingly beautiful dolls, which are perfect portrayals of femininity."*—BAW

The graceful and elegant Violet Waters is truly a team effort—Team Gene, that is. The café au lait vision was conceived and drawn by Mel Odom, the creator of the Gene doll; sculpted by Michael Evert, the artist who had previously collaborated with Odom to sculpt Gene; given the glamorous story line of a singer/actress during 1940s Hollywood by people such as The Ashton-Drake Galleries' writer Kirk Swenk; and dressed by designers like Jose de D'Saenz, Tim Kennedy and Lynne Day, who fashion sensational outfits for Violet's shapely 15½-inch figure.

Odom had come on the doll scene in a big way in 1995 with the debut of Gene, the vinyl fashion doll that

*Above: Violet, 15½ inches, vinyl, in "Torch Song" outfit by Jose D'Saenz; Opposite page: Violet in "Fascination" ensemble by Lynne Day*

The Ashton-Drake Galleries, the doll's manufacturer, hoped would give Barbie some serious competition. Odom, who was born in Richmond, Virginia, started out as a professional illustrator, earning the award of excellence from the Society of Illustrators and having his work exhibited in numerous museums. "I began drawing Barbie as a cultural icon, and in the process became more attracted to the idea of making my own icon. Looking back, it seems inevitable. The largest number of things that I enjoy connect in Gene and her friends—fashion, drawing, movies and storytelling. I couldn't resist.

"From the start I wanted Gene to have some friends," Odom continues. "Violet was in my mind for two or three years before she 'happened.' She was a long time coming. I saw something on television about the friendship between Ava Gardner and Lena Horne. When Ava Gardner got the part of Julie (a black character) in Showboat, Lena Horne—who should have gotten the part were it not for the reality of the Hollywood system of the time—helped Ava prepare for the part. I just thought that type of graciousness was amazing, and it inspired me." Odom presented the concept of Violet to Ashton-Drake executives and let it "percolate with them for a while." Every time someone would go up to him at shows and ask why he did not have an African-American doll, he would encourage them to take their question to the folks at Ashton-Drake. To their credit, they realized the authentic need and desire for such a doll, and they gave Odom the go-ahead. It was all Odom needed. He'd already been accumulating photos of models and black actresses of the period. Taking these with his own detailed drawings, Odom visited Evert and told him of his new project. Evert was all for it.

"I'm always glad to do a new character with Mel. He's so much fun to work with and has such a strong vision. He communicates what he wants clearly and kindly, so it's very easy for me to execute his ideas," says Evert.

Originally from Pittsburgh, Pennsylvania, Evert studied at the University of Pittsburgh and the Tyler School of Art in Rome, Italy. After moving to New York, where he now has a studio, he did jobs such as restorations, "ghost sculpting" and creating mannequins for companies, such as Pucci, which initially recommended

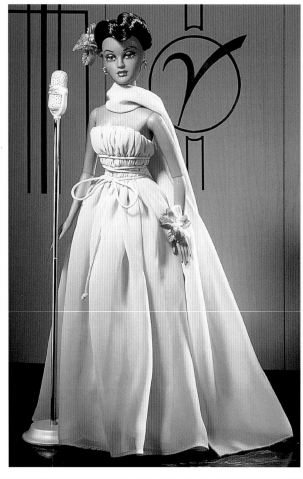

him to Odom. Since working with Odom, Evert has also done other doll projects for the Alexander Doll Company and Marie Osmond, and he is working on a doll prototype of his own.

Odom and Evert discussed Violet at length. Evert then went to work putting Odom's two-dimensional rendering into three-dimensional form. After Evert shaped an initial sculpt, he and Odom worked together to fine-tune the face and body. Evert often made changes on the spot based on Odom's specifications.

Odom was quite clear that Violet should not be a café au lait version of Gene, and consciously set about making her distinctive. "She's a singer and I wanted that to somehow be conveyed through her lips, which we made parted," Odom explains. "I also wanted her to have different hands. Violet's fingers are longer, and I think her hands are just the most beautiful. Three African-American ladies once came up to me at a show and one of the ladies looked at Violet's hands and said, 'Oh, she has piano-playing hands.' You don't know how great that made me feel. Violet is all about music.

"My dolls are very stylized; they look like my drawings and have fictional lives that are set in Hollywood during the 1940s and 1950s." Of Violet in particular Odom says, "I had many memories of beautiful black women in films, singing and being absolutely spellbinding. I went to those memories for Violet."

Violet premiered in 2001. Introduced simultaneously with male fashion doll Trent Osborn, Violet joined Gene Marshall and Madra Lord in The Gene Team Collection of fashion dolls from The Ashton-Drake Galleries. The Niles, Illinois-based company reproduces Odom's designs in vinyl, selling them for $79 to $100, depending on each doll's ensemble.

"With Violet, we wanted to accentuate the positives," Odom emphasizes. "If Gene is heart and Madra is emotion, then Violet is music. She is everything I wanted her to be—sweet, vulnerable and lovable. As with all my dolls, I want Violet to evoke feelings of optimism, comfort, joy and curiosity.

"Dolls like Violet are objects of beauty first; that is their job—being beautiful," Odom continues. "We bring our dreams to dolls, and they give them back to us in small bites we can swallow. They reassure us about ourselves. Violet, like Gene and Madra, are icons for a lot of people's lives. These dolls provide pleasure and a rush for people."

# LORNA PARIS

*"You have to be impressed with Lorna's enchanting dolls. Her innovative, hand-painted leather dolls with their radiant faces will give you joy. Highly collectible because of her brilliant artistry and design, these cuties are unrivaled."—BAW*

**66** I believe my dolls have healing power because I put so much love into them," says native New Yorker Lorna Paris. "In the summer I go to the ocean to work on the dolls. There is something very spiritual and peaceful there. Perhaps this feeling in me springs from my East Indian/Caribbean roots. I feel one with the Creator who gave me this wonderful ability to make dolls. I will make them until I am mentally or physically unable to do so anymore."

Not surprisingly Paris' attachment to dolls started early. "I first became interested in dolls as a child. My Aunt Winnie made my first black doll by hand—the doll was bigger than I was! She was beautiful with her embroidered face, black wool hair and store-bought clothes. My mother and other family members would always give me dolls. These became my little friends and playmates, as I was an only child.

"My mother was so creative; she could do almost anything in the arts…sewing, singing, designing, cooking. For years, she designed and made all my clothes. I dressed like a princess. I never thought I would be making dolls because I wanted to have a singing career like my mother. But my first doll that my Aunt Winnie made for me must have left a deeper impression on me than I had thought. Then there was the period in the 1980s when I used to sit and observe my friend Gregory design and make hats out of leather. The brilliant colors and prints on the leather fascinated me. The tans and shades of brown must have brought to mind the shades that human beings come in. There were times when I would even help Gregory in a crunch."

Pieces of Paris' life mosaic started fitting into place

*"Kali," 24 inches, leather*

Left: "Shanna," 8½ inches, suede leather;
Below left: "LuLu," 24 inches, leather strips;
Below: "Lorna's Bride," 8 inches, leather

in 1989, when the artist, unemployed and at a loss, began praying for guidance. She believes it came in the guise of the gift of a doll. "My friend Ka sent me a little cloth doll resembling me. He told me, 'Lorna, this doll will change your life.' It was this doll that gave me the motivation to design my own dolls." Already inspired by Gregory's leather-hat designs, she decided to use the pliable medium to make her own all-leather doll.

"From this time onwards, I would continuously use Gregory's leather scraps to improve my craft," Paris relates. "Once I'd completed the doll that made me proud of my toil, I felt encouraged that I'd accomplished my goals and dreams. My dolls continued to be my primary artistic focus, and are now like my family."

Paris' first doll sale was at a flea market at Manhattan's Fashion Institute of Technology. From there, she went on to sell her dolls in Harlem, where she met an African vendor who invited her to accompany him to a doll show in Connecticut. "It was on this trip, in 1990, that I met my representative, Bernice Gasaway. Bernice offered to take my dolls with her to the various shows to promote them. As soon as she'd lay the dolls out, dealers would buy them up. The demand surpassed my supply."

Ironically, a New York manufacturer had to travel to a Hong Kong Toy Show to discover the New York-based Paris' dolls. Later, he met her on her home turf and signed her up independently. Resulting from this contract, Paris' dolls were mass-produced in vinyl in 1994 by the Commonwealth Toy Company, and were sold worldwide in major department stores such as Toys 'R Us, Walmart and Venture Department Stores.

Today, Paris designs about twenty-five dolls a year. From eight to twenty-four inches high, most are one-of-a-kind pieces. "I love and get excited about creating a different doll each time out. Each creation inspires a new one," the artist says. "My rag dolls, made from leather and inspired by Raggedy Ann and Andy, I produce as limited editions of fifteen to twenty-five." Prices for her pieces begin at $200 and go up to about $2,500 for dolls, and $75 to $100 for wearable doll art.

About eighty-five percent of Paris' dolls portray black subjects. "My research is done on the move with eyes and ears open. I feel very lucky to be based in New York where the world is on parade," she says. "There are so many racial lines flowing into the 'Black Race' that variety in appearance is infinite. I do not approach my black subjects any differently than any other ethnic group. I see them as a part of the great family of man, unique in their being, and alike in their altogether. I make all my dolls to show the humanity and the glory of mankind."

*"Ranjana," 22 inches, leather*

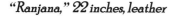

# DENITA NYREE PILTZER

*"To me, Denita celebrates the 'joy of creating' with exuberant energy.
Her dolls are most intriguing and dramatic. Her amazing doll artistry is
committed to excellence. Majestic and elegant best describe her creations,
for she creates beyond all expectations."—BAW*

Denita Nyree Piltzer's doll sculptures speak of the pride, tradition, courage and indomitable spirit at the heart of the African soul. Through her gifted hands and artistic vision, she creates a world populated with exotic singers, wandering nomads and legendary figures inspired from the collective consciousness of Africa's rich cultural diversity. Her self-declared goal is to "enlighten the viewer about history and instill a sense of pride in things African."

Although she was born in Colorado Springs, Colorado, Nyree Piltzer, the daughter of a military man stationed in numerous countries throughout his career, is a true child of the world. Perhaps because of her extensive travels, through her work she seems to seek to forge a kinship with, if not an actual place, a people, and to connect to a feeling of something permanent and binding that ties her to the comforting unity of a shared heritage.

With her dolls and the stories they tell, Nyree Piltzer is, in essence, coming home to her ancestral roots. Her own artistic roots began to blossom from the time she entered grade school. Starting when she was in the first grade, and all the way through high school, she won awards for her drawings and paintings. Her interest in dolls was always a presence as she continued collecting dolls— a happy by-product of her military dad's globe-trotting assignments—and "adopted" discarded dolls found at Salvation Army stores, which she would lovingly transform from unwanted orphans into beloved playmates by fixing their broken parts and fashioning new clothing and hairstyles for them.

While still in high school, Nyree Piltzer attended summer sessions at the San Francisco Art Institute and received

college credits for courses in figure drawing. Upon graduation, she attended the Institute for a full curriculum of illustration, design and sewing, which enabled her to become a fashion designer. In 1979, while living in Brooklyn, New York, Nyree Piltzer began making soft-sculpture dolls. After years of study, both in the United States and abroad, she combined various disciplines she'd mastered into her own distinctive style and established Tribal Art Dolls. The themes of the dolls Nyree Piltzer created under this banner stemmed from her deep love of her people's culture. Her first pieces were one-of-a-kind dolls; she went on to create small editions of five to ten. Her dolls are priced from $600 to $5,000.

Inspired by African history and books, especially photo books of Africa, all of Nyree Piltzer's realistic and detailed dolls are black. In 1982, upon her return to the San Francisco Bay area, she began to display and sell her creations at black doll shows and cultural events. By 1991 the artist was living in Paris, France; seeking a way to carry her art further, she began sculpting dolls in wax. Once back in America, Nyree Piltzer started making molds for her wax models from which she cast sculptures in resin. This enabled her to create original limited editions of her dolls. Today, a member of the Professional Doll Artists Guild and Millennium Doll Artistry, she continues to keep alive the history of her people and the art of the doll.

*Opposite page "Mali Singer,"
16 inches, resin; Right: "Nomad of
Niger," 22 inches, resin*

# Joy Roberts~Hill

*"Joy's philosophy is to bring happiness through her expressive dolls. With a delicate, unique artistic style, she presents traditional craftsmanship at its highest quality. Constantly striving to perfect her work, this artist deserves our utmost respect."—BAW*

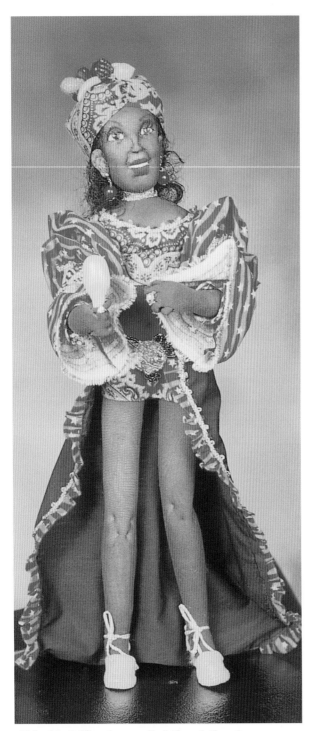

*"Matilda," 19 inches, stuffed fiber doll with wire armature and painted eyes*

**66** I have always had an interest in dolls, and started collecting them in 1989 to decorate my Christmas tree," relates Joy Roberts-Hill, who eventually came to have up to thirty dolls in her collection. Of these, only five were black. "I used to complain all the time about the scarcity of black dolls. Though I love all kinds of dolls, I've always felt that as a woman of color, I should have more than five black dolls in my personal collection."

Accordingly, in 1994 when her good friend Virginia Brown suggested the pair get together for informal arts and crafts sessions, Roberts-Hill was game to try her hand at making dolls of color. The pair was having so much fun and felt so good about their projects that Brown suggested they try selling them. "It was May of 1994 and Virginia expressed a desire to make cloth dolls to sell at craft shows. I was inspired and decided that if we were going to work on crafts, I would try my hand at dollmaking as well."

That same year the two budding doll crafters began to co-host their own doll shows in New York City. Knowing almost nothing about doll shows, the pair nevertheless persevered over many hurdles, learning a little bit more each time. Using the valuable lessons they gained, Brown formed GodsWay dolls in 1994, while Roberts-Hill established Doll-e-Mark in 1995. Now joined by her son and partner, John Peace—also an artist—Roberts-Hill's objectives are to "create beautiful dolls of color, to promote the work of striving artists, and to enrich the community by exhibiting and teaching dolls as art."

Roberts-Hill, who graduated from New York's Bronx Community College in 1993 with a degree in education, works as a secretary at Beth Israel Medical Center. But she's brought her love of dolls to her workplace in a unique way—twice a year, on her own time, she runs a free six-week doll therapy workshop for patients at Beth Israel's psychiatric outpatient clinic.

"I'm especially proud that I've been able to seek out and encourage young African-American women whose works have appeared in my shows and in other venues," says Roberts-Hill. "And the works of some of the [Beth Israel] patients have been exhibited at doll shows. My students really inspire me."

Roberts-Hill's dolls "incorporate history, personality and culture, which in years past were not traditionally reflected in ethnic dolls," she says. Her dolls—predominantly

one-of-kind soft sculptures priced from $125 to $600—depict the wide variety of skin tones, facial features and hair textures prevalent in people of color.

"I wanted to design cloth dolls unlike any I had seen, something I would desire for my own collection—cloth dolls that could stand next to the porcelain dolls in my collection and be equally admired for their beauty," says Roberts-Hill, who is a member of the Academy of American Doll Artists and has had her work exhibited at New York galleries, as well as in doll publications. "I didn't know how I would achieve this at the time, and I'm still working on it. As I learn more about how to make dolls, I feel I will some day accomplish my goal, which is to create cloth dolls that are realistic, beautiful and reflect the way I see my people."

# MARK E. RUFFIN

*"Enjoy an unforgettable doll experience: Mark's phenomenal dolls invite you on a magical trip into his doll kingdom, while you enrich your path to joy beyond all expectations."—BAW*

If you tune in to children's television shows produced by companies such as the Jim Henson Company and Walt Disney Enterprises, you'll most likely see some of the work of Emmy Award-winning designer Mark E. Ruffin.

"There is no greater satisfaction for me as an artist than to see the smile on children's faces when they gravitate to a doll that speaks directly to them," says the artist, who won his first Daytime Emmy for the 1993-94 season of Children Television Workshop's *Sesame Street*. "To watch kids hug and caress a doll that looks like them and that they have selected, that's a heartwarming, life-changing experience!"

Dolls played a central role in his own childhood. "There are photographs of me as early as the age of two holding a doll in my arms," says the artist who was born on September 22, 1962, in Philadelphia, Pennsylvania. "I come from a very creative family that nurtured my creativity by sharing and encouraging me in my own artistic expression."

Under his mother's instruction, Ruffin began to sew at the age of four. His great grandmother and grandmother furthered his education by instructing him in dressmaking and fine needlework. His father, an art teacher, gave Ruffin his first book on puppet making.

"As a child, there were those family members who would say things like 'boys don't play with dolls,' but even then, in my child's mind I would reason with myself and say 'but boys own the factories that make the dolls,'" notes Ruffin. Still intent on his personal road to doll success, by the age of fourteen, he was writing and producing his own theatrical performances at local public libraries, community centers and churches.

After graduating from high school, where he studied fine arts and industrial design, Ruffin attended the Fashion Institute of Technology in New York City, from which he earned an associate degree in fashion design. He began working as a puppet builder/designer with the Jim Henson Company in 1992.

"While working as a puppet builder with the Jim Henson Company, I began to experiment with various methods of dollmaking," Ruffin says. "I decided to follow my passion and began attending doll shows, first as a spectator, then as an artist. I entered the commercial doll world in 1998, becoming the first African-American designer for the Alexander Doll Company. The experience was priceless; it gave me the tools and resources to bring my own vision to fruition."

Perfecting his techniques for the past three decades, Ruffin has finely tuned his own approaches to traditional puppet and figure making. The artist, who sculpts anywhere from twenty-five to fifty dolls a year, works in porcelain, foam latex, clay, papier-mâché, wood, cloth, plastic and vinyl; his favorite is cloth because, as he explains, "there is just something very honest about cloth."

Most of Ruffin's designs begin as one of-a-kind pieces. Then if an idea is successful, he may choose to create others in a limited edition. The prices for his dolls, which range from ten to thirty inches in height, start at around $65 and go up to $500.

When it comes to creating, Ruffin does not necessarily think along color lines. "I don't know if I am drawn to portraying dolls of black characters per se," he explains. "I am just creating images in figurative form to reflect the people I encounter in life.

"For a long time there wasn't very much color in my work," Ruffin notes. "When you work in the commercial doll world there is an untruth, within some companies, that dolls of color don't sell. I may have believed that before going into the warehouses and seeing the mass quantities of returned dolls, none of which were of color. Because of my strong personal conviction pertaining to the power of positive images of every color, I choose to create figures that relate to my community first. From there I reach out to my neighbors around the globe to create images that are relevant to them."

His images have struck responsive chords in a wide audience. After winning his Emmy, he went on to earn four consecutive nominations for Outstanding Achievement in Costume Design. In 1995, Ruffin accompanied *Sesame Street* cast members to The White House to meet with then First Lady Hillary Rodham Clinton and discuss funding for children's educational programming.

Ruffin's work has appeared in Broadway shows, including *Cats*, *The Lion King* and *Phantom of the Opera*, and in Walt Disney theme parks. In addition, he has designed costumes for pop stars, rhythm-and-blues divas, movie stars and animated characters. The innovative

and multi-talented designer, who has conducted puppet-making workshops for children, has also contributed his talents to two books—*Muppets Make Puppets* and *The Muppets Big Book of Crafts*. In addition, in 2000, Seagram Americas chose him to create a piece to represent The City of Philadelphia for the ABSOLUT Africa Show. His commissioned piece was unveiled at the University of Pennsylvania Museum of Anthropology and Archeology, and it now resides in the ABSOLUT Museum in Sweden.

Describing himself as a perfectionist and an innovator, Ruffin explains, "I take great pride in my work and attempt to approach each figure, regardless of hue, with respect to its cultural background. The majority of my work is directed towards children, and children are the same all over the world; they just want to play, so for me it's most important that my works have kid appeal. It is my hope that my works convey happiness, joy and wonderment of life through the eyes of a child."

Ruffin's message to children of all ages and races: "Follow your passion and dreams in this life. The one thing that gives you the most happiness in life is your gift to share and you must because that is the part that is God-given."

# LORNA MILLER SANDS

*"We have grown to expect Lorna's dolls to be so precious and adorable that they captivate our hearts. We watch closely to see if they will cry or move. Because of their heartwarming appeal, they are today's treasures, providing us with lasting reminders of the joys of childhood."—BAW*

Lorna Miller Sands' "light-bulb moment" came in 1990 during a visit to Hamburg, Germany, when she spied some dolls that captured her creative fancy. "I had never seen dolls that looked so realistic before," the artist marvels. "I can't explain why the dolls made such an impact on me, especially considering the fact that until then I had had no interest in dolls. I guess it was meant to be."

Upon her return to the United States, the former telemarketer, whose artistry is completely self-taught, blithely went about creating her first dolls. "It didn't occur to me that I might need to read a book or take a class," she now recounts with a smile and shake of her head at her fearless faith that she'd be able "to just make it up as I went along."

It was a good thing she trusted her instincts. She labored and refined her skills over the course of several years. Today, more than a decade later, the artist has a well-established reputation for creating realistic black toddlers and children with engaging expressiveness. But it was only four years ago, when she started making incredibly life-like babies, that she felt as if she had finally come into her own. "With my precious babies life has truly not been the same," notes Miller Sands. "After making the switch to babies, everything is fresh, new and exciting! I just love creating these little ones! I knew there was a definite need in the market because I haven't seen many realistic babies, especially black ones. The collectors especially seem to love the skin tone, which I think is what is most realistic on my babies."

Varying from light-skinned cuddly bundles of joy to darker-skinned darlings, Miller Sands' creations are so life-like they often fool collectors, who mistake them for the real thing. And no wonder—Miller Sands' cuties feature hands and feet so detailed that you can actually see their wrinkles and the pink coloring in their palms, while the soles of their feet have the colorations of a real black baby. Even the tips of her dolls' ears are a bit darker than the surrounding area, just as they are on a real newborn.

Miller Sands, the mother of four, doesn't need to look far for inspiration or material. Her own children provide everything she needs—even contributing strands of their own hair, which Miller Sands painstakingly embeds into the clay heads of her dolls.

Designing about forty-eight dolls annually, Miller

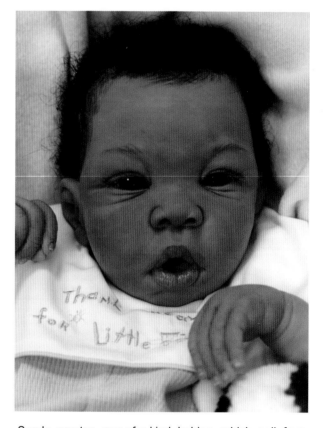

Sands creates one-of-a-kind babies, which sell from $2,300 to $4,000, as well as a line of three resin babies limited to thirty-five pieces each. These limited-edition pieces are priced from $500 to $700. In addition, Lee Middleton Original Dolls, Inc. began producing Miller Sands' babies in vinyl in January 2003. These babies range from eighteen to twenty-three inches in length and feature wire armatures and glass eyes.

"I have seen firsthand the impact that my babies have on people," says the talented Miller Sands with evident satisfaction and pride. "They've turned many frowns into smiles. I can't imagine anything better! I think I've found what I was supposed to be doing in life by sculpting babies."

*Above: "Nikolas," 21 inches, mixed media;*
*Opposite page: "Time Out," 18 inches, mixed media*

114

# ROTRAUT SCHROTT

*"Precious and beautifully sculptured, with incredibly appealing expressions, Rotraut's dolls invite us on an artistic journey of absolute realism. She endeavors to capture through her dolls not only the nature of children, but also the collective human experiences."—BAW*

Ask in-the-know doll connoisseurs about which doll artists and dolls come to mind when they think "black dolls," and the name and remarkable portrait dolls of German-born artist Rotraut Schrott invariably come up. Although only about twenty percent of her dolls are of black subjects (fifteen percent are of other minorities while the remaining sixty-five percent depict Caucasians), these former are so realistic and possess such beauty, grace and expressiveness that they stand apart even among the most distinguished of groups.

"I feel especially attracted to black faces and like to sculpt them because they allow for very strong expressions," says the artist, whose very first doll—created in 1981—was of a young black girl. "I was very proud of it," she recalls, "and I showed her with other artist dolls in my first exhibition." Since this auspicious start, Schrott's dolls have been included in numerous other major exhibits and doll shows around the world, and she's garnered many prestigious prizes and awards. She's also written *Making Original Portrait Dolls in Cernit*. From 1987 to 1997, she collaborated with the Rancho Mirage, California-based The Great American Doll Company (GADCO) to produce limited-edition dolls in porcelain and vinyl. These days, however, she creates only one-of-a-kind dolls. The dolls are priced from $4,500 to $10,000, and are from twenty-six inches to thirty-three inches high. On occasion, such as with the stunning "Black Madonna with Child," her statuesque figures can reach up to forty inches in height.

Schrott prefers to work in Cernit since she finds it a "material that radiates warmth, making faces seem as if they are breathing the air of life." Incredibly life-like down to the minutest detail—including the costuming, which the artist creates completely on her own—all of her work is meticulously crafted. This accounts for the fact that Schrott designs and sculpts only about eight to ten dolls a year.

The daughter of the well-known portraitist Ludwig Adam, Schrott grew up fascinated by the paintings of Old Masters like Boticelli, Rembrandt, Titian and Velazquez. So, when she began designing dolls, it was only natural that this admiration would spill over and influence her own work. "All my efforts are aimed at sculpting the faces to capture the delicate fineness, soft-cut features and warm expressions that I admire so

*Above: "Inono," 31½ inches, Cernit; Opposite page: "Black Madonna with Child," 40 inches, Cernit*

much from the works of the Old Masters," she notes.

"I never want my dolls to be just decorations or figures of fantasy. I want them to be like living creatures you might meet in the street at any time," says Schrott, who has a special fondness for representing children. The mother of three grown children, she delights in portraying the myriad expressions of young boys and girls discovering the world and all its wonders. For instance, with "Dreaming Angel" the artist has masterfully realized her aim of sculpting a little black girl imagining the celestial joys of earning her wings. "Her expression seems to say 'it's wonderful,'" says Schrott, "and I think I managed to convey her facial features in such a way that the collector can read and feel this little girl's thoughts." With

"Charlize," a sweetly proper young girl dressed in a pretty white frock, Schrott has sought—and achieved—the goal of conveying a sense of "the harmony between the face and body language."

With "Inono," a piece created in 2002, the mood is one of gentleness and sensitivity to nature and God's smallest creatures. Like all her work, these endearing figures invoke us to embrace and rejoice in the universal emotions that bind us all in our common humanity.

*Below: "Dreaming Angel," 33 inches, Cernit*
*Opposite page: "Charlize," 34 inches, Cernit*

# LuLu Tatum

*"LuLu creates a love for nostalgia in her dolls. Bringing out old-fashion charm, her dolls are a reflection of yesteryear. Artistically, LuLu successfully captures every child's vivid expression and solemn innocence. Classically, LuLu's dolls will become a legacy for tomorrow's collectors."—BAW*

Whether portraying a pensive expression in a doll like "Liberty" or the radiant joy found in her darling "Beloved Belindy," LuLu Tatum captures a moment in time with skillful sensitivity and empathy. Her affection for her subjects and her medium is as clear as the artistry involved in bringing them to fruition. "I really don't know exactly when I started loving dolls, because as far back as I can remember, I always had one in my arms," Tatum says. "I was a definite tomboy who loved being outdoors, but I always had a doll right next to me. My mother and both grandmothers were seamstresses, and they made me so many dolls. One of my grandmothers even showed my sister and me how to make dolls out of flowers, twigs and leaves. We would play with them for hours! My sister and I were also taught how to sew, crochet and knit, so we spent many, many hours making clothes for our dolls.

"I cannot recall a time I wasn't doing some kind of artistic project; it's just been that way my whole life. I've always loved the study of all different kinds of people of various sizes, color and ages. I never cease to be amazed at the beauty of all of the different cultures and languages. As a result of that great love, most of my art-work, whether it is a painting, sculpture or doll, has a 'people' character. I discovered sculpting dolls in the 1980s, and a whole new world opened up for me because, not only was I able to sculpt, but I could put my sculpt on a poseable body, and then make a costume, and I absolutely love to sew!"

Tatum has made dolls representing almost all races and cultures, but black dolls are her mainstay. "I love all possibilities available to me when planning the sculpt of a black doll," she notes. "There is so much history—good and bad—so there is so much to work from for per-sonalities, expressions, etc. Whether they are happy, sad, curious or in serious thought, all my ethnic dolls have proud expressions. I probably do more research for my black dolls, especially if they are from a different

country, to make sure that my creation is as accurate as possible.

"I love creating subjects from either long ago, or from far away," Tatum continues. "I have made very few modern-type dolls. I tend to start sculpting a doll that has a story to tell. When you look into their eyes, I want more than anything for you to feel they have a soul. I also love the natural fabrics from yesteryear. Most of the fabrics I use on my dolls are from antiques I have collected, and the same goes for the shoes and accessories I use. When I create a doll from another country, I try to use fabrics and styles from that particular part of the world. I always use my hands as models and when I work on the palms, they have my lines, and I have a long lifeline."

Although she also creates popular small, limited-

edition resins in one-of-a-kind outfits and a wonderful selection of artist bears sculpted with leather faces, Tatum is best known for her one-of-a-kind Cernit dolls dressed in vintage clothing. Depending on their size, these dolls usually start at $1,200 and go up to $8,000. Many of her dolls have sold to well-known collectors, and they are spread around the globe. "My dolls are living in many foreign countries, and I receive mail all the time from the owners, who keep me up to date on how my creations are doing," she relates with evident satisfaction.

*Above: "Beloved Belindy," 32 inches, lumicast resin; Opposite page, left: "Sophie Mae," 32 inches, Cernit; Far left: "Liberty," 29 inches, lumicast resin*

*"Gloria's dolls are wonderfully modeled and exhibit a multitude of expressions, revealing her sensitivity to children. Her dolls are so desirable because they are unsurpassed in beauty."—BAW*

**"M**y dolls are unique, but what makes them unique I cannot say," notes Gloria Tepper. Luckily, she has no need to say more. Her delightful creations speak for themselves.

Originally a designer of decorative fabrics, Tepper began making dolls in the mid 1990s. "I saw my first wax antique dolls in a store while waiting for an appointment and felt in my gut and hands that I could do it," she says of the decisive moment that was to change the course of her professional path. With dolls, Tepper discovered her ideal artistic form. "If you find your best skill is sculpting and you don't have the means to be a 'Sculptor,' dolls provide the perfect alternative. They bring me tremendous satisfaction. With them I know I can use whatever artistic skills are at my disposal."

Although she now says it was "technically a mistake; I should have taken every course available," Tepper taught herself dollmaking through trial and error. After struggling for two years and experimenting with different mediums such as kiln-fired water-based stoneware clay and porcelain, she finally found her way. Today she feels most comfortable working with stoneware clay because it is a direct-sculpture medium that requires no molds. At first, she made limited-edition dolls, but all too quickly found herself bored and unfulfilled with the monotony of repeatedly turning out the same doll. So, with her husband's loving support, she opted to follow her creative impulses wherever they would lead her.

A keen observer of life and faces, Tepper had only to step outside her door and into the marvelous ever-flowing stream of inspirations that passed her on the streets of her native New York. Sometimes it was a child photographed in a playground, caught in a moment of pure glee as her mother tossed her in the air, sometimes it was a young girl with unforgettable blue eyes shining out of a creamy café au lait profile, or it could be a Currier and Ives-type print of street kids playing marbles. Whatever the subject matter, or the inspiration behind it, all her works radiate with humanity.

"I wanted to inject a life force into my pieces," Tepper asserts. "I wanted them to have an overall completeness. I wanted them to answer questions and to

*Right: "Henry," 28 inches, kiln-fired stoneware; Opposite page: "Kadida," 29 inches, kiln fired stoneware*

make a statement. People who own my dolls get pleasure from them. They are not commercial cop-outs or imitations of what I have seen before."

In order to give each piece the attention she feels it merits, Tepper now prefers to limit her yearly production to eight one-of-a-kind pieces and limited-edition porcelain pieces of no more than twenty-five. About eighty-five percent of her dolls are black characters. "What attracted me to making black dolls was the sculptural beauty of the faces, the warmth and depth of expression and the freedom not to imitate dolls of the past," Tepper explains.

"I respond more to the expressiveness of black faces and the sculptural forms I see there," she notes of her pieces, which start at $3,500 and range in height from twenty-four to twenty-nine inches. "My black dolls are the best pieces of art I have ever made, and I enjoy making them."

*"Alicia," 28 inches, porcelain*

# ROBERT TONNER

*"The evocative, exquisite designs of Robert Tonner's dolls present us with stunning depictions of romantic and timeless beauty. Expressing every emotion that is the essence of womanhood in dolls, their quality is encapsulated with elegance and glamour."—BAW*

Robert Tonner, who was born in Bluffton, Indiana, was a small-town boy with big dreams that have come true and taken him down unexpected paths he never envisioned. Always creative and artistic, he started out to pursue a career in the fashion world. After graduating from Parsons School of Design in New York City with a B.F.A. degree, he worked for the sportswear company Gamut and for Bill Blass. Thanks to his design talents, he quickly rose to head the Blassport label and by 1983 he could boast his own label—Robert Tonner for Tudor Square.

About this same time, Tonner was also finding personal satisfaction and deriving much more enjoyment from his pursuit of doll collecting and early attempts at doll sculpting. Through friendships he made in doll circles, he was becoming more and more immersed in this fun and novel community, and as the business politics and financial stresses of his full-time career grew greater, the doll world beckoned as an increasingly tempting alternative.

After losing financial backing for Tudor Square and going back to being employed by others in a series of unfulfilling and frustrating fashion jobs, Tonner made the gutsy move to launch his doll company in 1991. A year later, at the American International Toy Fair in New York City, he debuted his fashion dolls to great acclaim. Steadily and surely, he has grown the Hurley, New York-based company into a highly successful and respected enterprise, and along the way earned the admiration, respect and support of other doll artists, the media and collectors. In 2002, his company purchased the Effanbee Doll Company, and he is now working with a talented team to inject new ideas and managerial savvy to "reintroduce some of Effanbee's decades-loved vintage products with significant updates and a totally new design perspective."

Tonner's business acumen, personal charm and "nice guy" reputation have garnered him much respect. In 1988 he was elected into the National Institute of American Doll Artists (NIADA)—he served as the prestigious organization's president from 1995-1997—and his work has recently been displayed at the Museum of Decorative Arts at the Louvre in Paris, France.

*"Urban Sport Esmé," 16 inches, vinyl/hard plastic*

125

Tonner Doll Company's slogan is "believe in the power of play." And the artist's creations, which range from sweet-faced children to gorgeous fashion dolls, are characterized by a "play-doll style" to which he brings a classic, idealized aestheticism with a strong infusion of fashion razzle dazzle.

"I'm mostly interested in portraying beauty," Tonner emphasizes. "I create dolls that I feel are beautiful. When I create a doll like Emme (a full-figured fashion doll based on the real-life fashion model and celebrity of the same name) or Esmé (an African-American fashion doll from Tonner's Tyler Wentworth line), I am not really seeking to make any type of 'political' statement. I am primarily driven and inspired by a personal vision of beauty. To me, Emme is beautiful; the black models that I worked with during my fashion days and who served as inspiration for Esmé and some of my other African-American dolls are beautiful."

Of his Esmé doll, Tonner says, "There is so much to explore with the color richness of her skin tone; it opens up so many exciting design possibilities. I can experiment and work with colors and fabrics that go from being 'OK' on a white model to 'wow' against Esmé's skin tones. I find this very inspiring."

Rather than basing his work on photographs or any one actual person, Tonner works from a "collective ideal based on reality" to create his black dolls. Not surprisingly, fashion plays a major inspirational role in their conception. For instance, the impetus for "Olivia," one of Tonner's first African Americans in the American Model collection, came from a fabulous fabric. "I found an African print and fell in love with the bold colors and prints," Tonner notes. Limited to 500 pieces, the eighteen-inch vinyl doll with rooted hair and painted eyes is dressed in a gown of authentic African print cotton, with a matching stole and gold-tone accessories.

"Urban Sport Esmé" stood out in Tonner Doll Company's fashion doll line because of her trend-setting and stylish micro braids, and the fact that Tonner does very few dolls in fashion pants outfits. The sixteen-inch beauty is striking in a vest of silver silk and metal broadcloth with a matching quilted topper coat over matching matte jersey leggings. "I wanted to do something very modern and urban for Esmé," Tonner comments of this design. One thing is for sure: No matter what she wears, Esmé—like her designer himself—never fails to make a memorable fashion statement.

*Opposite page: "Bronze Siren Esmé," 16 inches, vinyl/hard plastic; Right: "Olivia," 18 inches, vinyl*

# SHARON E. TUCKER

*"Capturing all the laughter and joy of childhood, Sharon's bodacious and mischievous dolls invite you into the incredible world of make-believe and magic. She is a serious doll artist for the young and young at heart."—BAW*

Sharon E. Tucker definitely has a flair with fabrics. One look at her colorful and delightful cloth creations, and you're drawn into her world of whimsical fun and fancy.

If her collectors are so attracted to them, it's largely because Tucker's characters fairly shout with the artist's own strong and compelling infatuation for them. "I came to have a true love for the art form. I do other things, but my heart belongs to the dolls," she says, with a true lover's fervor.

Tucker, who has been making dolls for about ten years, knows firsthand the draw of the doll from a collector's standpoint. In fact, that's what initially pulled her into the world of dollmaking. "I was browsing a yard sale about twelve years ago and a woman was selling her doll collection," Tucker explains. "I fell in love with one of her original-artist dolls. At the time, my children were young and I could not afford her asking price. So, after dreaming about the doll for several nights, I went to a crafts store and attempted to make my own version. My first creations were disasters, but I loved making dolls so I stuck with it. Slowly, I started to improve."

Today Tucker, who was born and still lives in Philadelphia, Pennsylvania, devotes herself to dollmaking full time. About ninety-five percent of her dolls, she says, are black or African American. "As an African-American artist, I first seek what I know. And second, I feel a need to pass on a little of our culture," she notes by way of explanation. All of Tucker's dolls are one-of-a-kind pieces. Each face is individually painted or sculpted, although the basic body—also designed by Tucker—-may stay

*Right: "Biscuit Boy," 24 inches, cloth doe suede and cloth; Opposite page: "Biscuit Girl," 24 inches, cloth doe suede and cloth*

the same. Prices for her dolls start at around $275 and go up to $850. They range in size from eight to twenty-nine inches. About fifty to seventy-five are "easy" designs like rag dolls, while five to ten involve more detailed designs such as needle-sculpted clowns and Santas.

Tucker describes her style as "eclectic, whimsical and most definitely colorful. I'm set apart by the humor of my work." Hoping her creations evoke smiles and a sense of joy, the dollmaker says, "I try to create a bit of whimsy in their expressions—especially the facial features. For example, I may over-exaggerate the noses or lips. I always give my dolls nicknames that have typically been used as 'pet' names in many African-American families. I enjoy putting on the finishing touches, adding the embellishments. It brings the doll to life."

Typical of her dolls—all of which have a signature tiny mole on their chin similar to the artist's own beauty mark—are pieces such as "Strummin'," "Biscuit Girl" and "Jazzy."

*Left: "Strummin'," 20 inches, cloth; Opposite page: "Jazzy," 20 inches, cloth doe suede and cloth*

# BETS & AMY VAN BOXEL

*"Astonishingly realistic, the van Boxels' child dolls are kindred souls to be cherished. They are fascinating and offer unparalleled remembrances from childhood of around the world."—BAW*

Bets van Boxel and her daughter Amy van Boxel share a unifying artistic endeavor that's just as strong as their blood ties. Whether working together or independently, they create beautifully sensitive portrayals of multicultural children. The common factor in all their work is the humanity and boundless intensity of the maternal instinct to nurture, love and celebrate the life of a child, whether it be their children, the offspring of their psyches or any of the many children of the world.

They might be relative newcomers to the American doll market, but between them these Dutch artists have had a lifetime of experience. Bets clocks in with more than thirty years, while Amy, who was born on April 2, 1968, can "officially" lay claim to seven years, even more if you consider all her formative training. ("As a child I would sit next to my mother and try to make a doll of my

own," Amy offers, adding she also often assisted her mother at doll exhibitions abroad.)

It seems the van Boxel women come to their artistic calling early in life. Bets, who was born on April 7, 1942, in Waspik, the Netherlands, worked as a seamstress from the age of fourteen; during the evenings she took classes in portrait and model painting. Upon marrying Jos van Boxel, she began spending more time taking classes at a local community center. "The people who sat before me were sometimes so interesting that I wanted to make them three-dimensional. The first doll I did was of a hobo I saw. I wanted to personify the expression on this man's face and show all the details of his clothing and possessions."

While Bets focused on her painting lessons, Jos was a few rooms away taking ceramics classes. This was to serve them both well after the couple entered into another partnership—the dollmaking company of De Poppenstee, where Jos now helps out by making his wife's doll molds.

Amy, who has a background in industrial design, joined the company in 1997 when her parents needed an assistant. Recently, she's started to create her own collection of porcelain dolls, which are limited to five each and range in size from four to sixteen inches.

Like the close-knit family they are, the van Boxels work to make their venture a success. Bets sculpts the dolls' heads, hands, feet and shoulder plates; Jos makes the molds and pours the porcelain; and Amy helps her mother sand and paint the porcelain pieces. While Jos and Amy sponge the paint on the doll parts, Bets does all the delicate work and all of the dolls' costuming.

Avid travelers, the van Boxels take inspiration from the children they encounter on their trips to exotic places. They not only soak up the local faces, expressions and "souls" of the people they visit, but also bring back doll fabrics, jewelry and other uniquely indigenous accessories with which to enhance their dolls.

Although her early pieces were one-of-a-kind dolls made from a self-hardening clay, Bets started working in porcelain in 1986 and now works only in it. "Porcelain

*Left: "Kakra & Fata" by Bets van Boxel, 20 inches, porcelain; Opposite page: "Mayan & Yapoyo" by Bets van Boxel, 33 inches, porcelain*

Above: "Sana" by Bets van Boxel, 23 inches, porcelain; Opposite page, left: "Joli" by Bets van Boxel, 12 inches, porcelain; Top right: "Mimi" by Amy van Boxel, 15 inches, porcelain; Bottom right: "Buzayan" by Amy van Boxel, 15 inches, porcelain

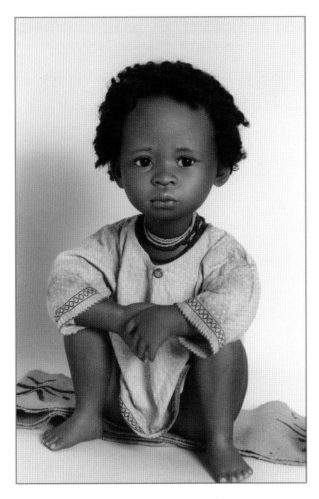

survives through centuries and has the right 'skin' for my dolls," says the artist, who currently designs two collections a year, each of which consists of six to ten dolls in limited editions of five. The dolls, which range from fourteen to thirty-three inches in height, sell for between $1,400 and $3,800. Bets also designs Basket Babies, soft-bodied dolls that come in little baskets and are usually limited to editions of ten.

There is a black doll in almost each of Bet's collections. "I'll sometimes make a white child, but only of one of my three grandchildren; the rest are of minorities," Bets explains. "I am inspired by the children that I meet on my trips. I could be inspired by a look in the eyes, a posture or their special ethnic clothing.

"My artistic style is very detailed and life-like," Bets elaborates. "I try to portray the people and children as they really are. I hope that people recognize something in my dolls that touches them like it touched me when I saw these children."

Amy—now a mother herself—shares her mother's artistic muses as well. All of the younger van Boxel's dolls thus far have had ethnic themes. Describing her style as "down-to-earth with a high reality factor," Amy notes, "I've made dolls inspired by children from Burma, Australia (aboriginal), Ghana, Vietnam and Tibet. My dolls are dressed in authentic clothing, but often with a touch of something modern. What attracts me to each ethnic group is not only the differences in the colors of the skins, but also their bone structure, posture, expression and way of dressing. To succeed in capturing the true form of every subject I create, I study each face, the nuances in the skin shades, the skull, the body and clothing. When I'm finished, I hope that the expression comes across and that people smile or look sad, that they feel what the doll feels."

# MARCELLA WELCH

*"'Marcella is a modern griot of spiritual consciousness and artistic visions. The creation of her beautiful dolls is a message of African continuity. Embracing ancestral roots, Marcella's dolls integrate sculpture and art into transforming power."—BAW*

Marcella Welch has been creating mixed-media art for more than twenty-five years. "In my role as an artist, I create clothing, jewelry, paintings and dolls. My work reflects my mixed cultural heritage of African, Native-American Indian and European blood," she says. "Most of my creative energy is geared towards the creation of dolls. I make them in all shades, from the light vanilla of my father to the darkest brown of my mother. I say through my work what I hesitate to say verbally."

Welch's pieces, which have been shown in several prestigious exhibitions—some of which traveled to the Smithsonian Institution in Washington, D.C., and the American Crafts Museum in New York City—are intensely personal statements. "When I make a doll, I am sharing a part of my life with the viewer," she confesses. "I'm telling a story about my life and the lives of other women. I fashion shapes to reflect our proud and fearless nature. I sometimes give them wings to denote our ability to overcome the worst adversities."

Describing them as "spirit dolls or figurative pieces," Welch explains, "at times my work is bold and sassy with colors and embellishments; at other times, my work is classy and subdued."

When she started making dolls professionally to sell, she was using a needle-sculpting technique. At first she fashioned white dolls because those were what sold best. For major art shows, she started making life-size soft sculptured dolls in vintage clothing. These were also extremely popular. However, in 1981, after all of her dolls were stolen, she lost her enthusiasm for life-size dolls, shifting instead to smaller, more Afro-centric pieces.

"In the 1980s, there was a renaissance of African-American art. It seemed that African-American artists were showing off their own style of creativity everywhere," recalls Welch. "Black artists were designing clothing, furniture, jewelry and so much more. Many of us wanted to be surrounded by art that reflected our culture and lifestyle. The art was bold, sassy and exciting. I wanted to make art for home décor, so I started making my art dolls so they would hang on walls. This one move

*Left: "Praise Dancer," 24 inches, paperclay and gourd; Opposite page: "The Offering," 24 inches, cut and painted gourd*

*Left: "Earth Spirit in Chair," 36 inches, cloth and paperclay; Opposite page, left: "Bird of Peace," 26 inches, Cernit head and cloth/wood body; Right: "Praise," 24 inches, painted clay face, gourd body with wire and paperclay arms and legs*

totally changed the way I marketed and sold my work. My first dolls in this genre were named 'Nubian Dancers.' Their bodies were made of black polished cotton with dresses of authentic West African fabrics. These were my most popular dolls and I sold hundreds of them."

Currently, Welch makes about one hundred dolls each year which are priced between $80 and $500. She creates both one-of-a-kind pieces and limited editions of ten to twenty-five dolls, mostly of black women. "I don't do traditional dolls, so I am free to portray my black figures as dancers, angels and spiritual guides."

Admitting that she does not do much research, Welch says her figures seem to take shape from accumulated life experience. "I have traveled to Brazil, West Africa and South Africa," she notes. "I've collected textiles, beads and found objects from many places. I've studied with other artists and teachers. I sew, paint, hand dye textiles, sculpt and bead. When I start to work on a new piece, all the materials and knowledge just seem to meld together.

"I hope to tell real stories with the dolls that I do. When you see one of my dolls, you see part of a visual map of my life. Each piece starts as an idea that may be expanded on before it comes into fruition. During this time period, which may consist of a few days or a few years, I mentally gather bits and pieces of ideas, fabrics, beads and found objects that will go into the final piece. By the time I go into the studio to work, I already have a mental picture of what I want my new creation to be. I have never been able to separate my emotions from my work. Indeed, there have been times when the grief in my life has caused me to stop working completely. It is at these times that I become retrospective. I contemplate what makes me gravitate towards making dolls and spend time daydreaming about new images I want to create. After this period of 'creative rest,' my work seems to have new life and vibrancy.

"A bit of my soul is imbued in each doll," Welch concludes. "The dolls are griots or storytellers, shamans, silent messengers. The dolls are me."

# PAULA WHALEY

*"Paula's understanding of human experiences is obvious in her innovative dolls, in their spirituality and grace. These mixed-media pieces, evoking both emotion and elegance in fluid form, are whispers of things past and future."—BAW*

Paula Whaley's work is born of equal parts of love and loss. Indeed, Whaley, who has been working in the creative arena for more than twenty years, credits her artistic evolution to the pain of losing her beloved older brother, James Arthur Baldwin, the highly acclaimed author and playwright, who died in 1987.

Whaley channeled her grief and the depth of feelings it engendered into her abundant creativity to give rise to a nurturing wellspring that has fed and healed her, and touched many of her collectors with a similar positive force. "In considering the art of healing, honesty can be both painful and therapeutic," she remarks. "At this particular time and space, my doll sculptures reflect intense personal moments and memories. I try always to celebrate the moment and enter into my own inner world—creative-ly—in order to be productive, alive and free."

Whaley, who is a graduate of the Fashion Institute of Technology in New York City and has furthered her studies at Cadres Couture in Paris, France, first began expressing her design talent with clothing, hats and jewelry. Gradually, this ever-evolving seeker of self-expression moved on to "soft sculptures" composed of clay, wood, metal and fabric. She adopted the professional name Oneeki (pronounced Oh-nee-kai), which is a feminine Yoruba name that means "treat her tenderly for me." And that is precisely the type of emotions she hopes her evocative pieces engender in their viewers.

"If my work can bring peace and harmony and uplift the spirit in each individual who views it," she declares, "then I have succeeded."

*Left: "Wisdom," 20 inches (seated), air-dry clay and cloth; Opposite page: "Aunt Bulah," 42 inches. clay head and hands with cloth body (Artist's photo: Ann Naito Haney)*

The youngest of the nine children of Berdis and David Baldwin, Whaley grew up in a poor family in Harlem, New York. However, her life was abundant with inspirational influences—her childhood and adolescent experiences, New York's rich cultural melting pot, and, most significantly, the role model of her eldest brother, whose essays, novels and plays vibrate with human emotion. Empowered by all of these positive factors, Whaley went on to explore her own creative path.

Collectors and art critics alike have lauded her highly individualistic style. Denise Barnes of *The Washington Times*, has commented: "Her art transforms clay into commentaries on society's ills, infusing her creations with a humanity and honesty as searing as the observations of her late brother, novelist James Baldwin."

Whaley's compelling sculptures, many of them fashioned of metal and fabric, are archetypical forms that evoke the majesty, grace and beauty of the proud people of the Masai and Fulani of Africa.

Today Whaley resides and works in Baltimore, Maryland. Her thought-provoking spiritual characters—frequently standing forty inches tall—have faces marked with life's often tragic and harsh passing, yet they also possess broad shoulders on which to bear their burdens. For no matter how hard their realities, how bleak their past or present, Whaley's characters seem to radiate with the quiet dignity and unconquerable will of the survivor who looks adversity in the face and does not stand down.

# GOLDIE WILSON

*"Goldie's knowledge and ceaseless exploration of the creative process give expressive charm and personality to her dolls. Portraying both vulnerability and innocence, Goldie's dolls are so irresistible that they leave a lasting impression while winning your heart."—BAW*

Born in 1938 in Birmingham, Alabama, Goldie Wilson started making dolls at the age of five when her grandmother, a seamstress who firmly believed that a "child had to be able to do something useful," taught her to sew and cut patterns for clothes. By the time she was seven, Wilson was also accomplished at embroidering, crocheting and knitting. In high school, the budding artist pursued her creative tendencies in art classes, where she learned to paint and draw. From there, she progressed to ceramics, ultimately starting her own shop, Goldie's Ceramics, where she taught classes for twenty-three years. Always looking for new creative avenues, she took classes herself in china painting and began making porcelain reproduction dolls in the late 1980s.

"I had always been interested in making dolls, but kept putting it off," she says. "Until one day I said to myself 'this is it,' and enrolled in a dollmaking class."

When she sculpted "Diamond," her first original doll, Wilson felt she had realized her dreams. Here, at last, was the culmination of all her skills and aspirations through which she could share parts of herself with the world. "Dolls are my little people, and through them I express all my emotions—sadness, happiness, joy, whatever I am feeling at the time I start to sculpt."

Today Wilson's dolls are completely her own. Making about five dolls a year, she sculpts them from original molds, and designs and assembles everything from the clothing to the jewelry, the shoes to the wigs. She prefers working in Earthware Clay because she finds it pliable and easy to shape.

Her heritage is a primary source of inspiration. "Being black, I had noticed a shortage of good African-American dolls relating to our everyday life," she says about her decision to concentrate on portraying only black dolls.

Wilson feels she's developed a style uniquely her own. "When you see a Goldie's doll, you will know it by the way I design and style the hair," she notes. "The sculpting of the face is representative of our different features. The coloring of the porcelain, the way I design and dress my dolls, these are what you might say are my signature marks."

Wilson creates mostly limited-edition dolls that number from two to twenty pieces. They typically cost about $895 each. In addition, she makes special-edition dolls for the Home Shopping Network, which began producing and selling her dolls in 2002.

Hard-pressed to find an aspect of dollmaking that she doesn't like, she says, "I love to sculpt. I love to see my doll's face come to life after I have sculpted and painted and put it together. I hope people will see my dolls as a joy and a comfort, something that's a beautiful piece of life, which they can look forward to when they come home. That's the exciting part. Oftentimes, you can't tell how the doll is going to look until it is completed. Sometimes she'll be pretty, other times, not. But one thing will be for sure—I put my heart and soul in my dolls, and I think it shows."

*Left: "Starr," 24 inches, porcelain with cloth body; Opposite page: "Namdi," 24 inches, porcelain with cloth body*

# Directory of Artists

Audrey Bell & Georgette Taylor
Big, Beautiful Dolls
70 Elm St.
West Orange, NJ 07052
973-669-3728
ajbell34@aol.com
www.bigbeautifuldolls.com

Floyd Bell
4572 Don Felipe Dr.
Los Angeles, CA 90008
323-296-3055
belledolls@msn.com

Sandra Miller Blake
109 Lake Stephen Lane
Blythewood, SC 29016
803-786-6904
smblake@worldnet.att.net
www.sodollightfuldolls.com
www.sandrablake.com

Martha Boers & Marianne
Reitsma
Martha and Marianne
1901 Malden Crescent
Pickering, Ontario
Canada L1V 3G3
reitsma@mac.com
marthaandmarianne.com

Anna Abigail Brahms
61 Gothic St.
Northampton, MA 01060
Abigail.brahms@verizon.net

Uta Brauser
23 Backroad
Madrid, NM 87010

Barbara Thiery Buysse
9630 Almena Rd.
Kalamazoo, MI 49009
269-375-3804
fm43@chartermi.net

Jennifer Canton
137 Bridle Path
Staunton, VA 24401
540-886-3737
canton@intelos.net
www.jennifercanton.com

Rosie Chapman
a.k.a. Miz Rosie
57325 Beaconsfield
Washington Twp., MI 48094
586-781-2970
mizrosie@sprynet.com
www.mizrosie.com

Patricia Coleman-Cobb
The Cobblestone Collection
2430 Castlemaine Ct.
Duluth, GA 30097
770-622-2172
Lcobbster@aol.com

Jodi and Richard Creager
3545 Bali Dr.
Lake Havasu, AZ 86406
www.creagers.com

Brigitte Deval
Pod Casanova 18
Trequanda 53020
Siena, Italy
39-0577-662201
dolls@bdeval.com

Tonia Mitchell Floyd
T.Rific! Characters
100 Tahoe Dr.
Fayetteville, GA 30214
770-716-0908
toniafloyd@yahoo.com
www.toniafloyd.com

Elissa Glassgold
3 Surrey Rd.
Elkins Park, PA 19027
eglassgold@comcast.net

Hildegard Günzel
Porzellanpuppenmanufaktur
Dr.-Alfred-Herrhausen-Allee 60
D-47228 Duisburg
Germany
011 49 2065 66199
designby@hildegardguenzel.com
www.hildegardguenzel.com

Philip Heath
Philip Heath Designs CB,
C/. Andrés Mancebo, 40, bajo, izq,
46023 Valencia
Spain
heathspain@netscape.net
www.philipheathdolls.com

Annette Himstedt
Annette Himstedt
Puppenmanufaktur
Karl-Schurz-Str.27
D-33100 Paderborn
Germany
01149 5251 521 70
mail@annettehimstedt.com
www.annettehimstedt.com

Doug James
DLD International
498 West End Ave., Suite 11D
New York, NY 10024
586-336-0758
www.dldintdoll.com

Kor January
3545 Haven St.
Cincinnati, OH 45220
513-559-1755
www.korjanuary.com

Elizabeth Jenkins
8203 NW Oregon Dr.
Kansas City, MO 64151
816-589-0573
jenkart@hotmail.com

Helen Kish
Kish & Company
1800 West 33rd Ave.
Denver, CO 80211
303-972-0053
kishco@msn.com

Susan Krey
15212 N. E. 195th St.
Woodinville, WA 98072
425-806-0184
Susan@Kreydolls.com
www.Kreydolls.com

Lisa Lichtenfels
PO Box 90537
Springfield, MA 01139
lisalichtenfels@aol.com

Chris Malone
c/o Angie's Doll Boutique
1114 King St.
Alexandria, VA 22314
703-683-2807

Doris McGillan
Heritage Designs
725 Westcroft Pl.
West Chester, PA 19382
610-399-0753
heritagedoll@juno.com

Pauline Middleton
Pauline Middleton Original Dolls
108 Lohr Ave.
Inverloch 3996
Victoria, Australia
011-61-35674-1135
pmdolls@tpg.com.au
www.pmdolls.com.au

Linda Murray
Doll Cottage
168a Nine Mile Ride
Finchampstead
Wokingham, Berkshire, RG40
4JB
Great Britain
011-44-118-973-4136
linda@lindamurray.co.uk
www.lindamurray.co.uk

Anne Myatt
Like Me Dolls
6910 Cypress Point Dr.
Houston, TX 77069
281-580-8005
justlikemedolls@att.net
www.likemedolls.com

Shirley Nigro-Hill
Shirley Nigro-Hill Originals
c/o Reverie Publishing Company
130 Wineow Street
Suite 3
Cumberland, MD 21502

Mel Odom
Star Blue Studio
2112 Broadway, #412
New York, NY 10023
Michael Evert's Studio:
212-533-9130

Lorna Paris
Leather Doll Creations
474 West 144th St., Suite 9
New York, NY 10031
646-456-3323

Denita Nyree Piltzer
215 Masonic Ave.
San Francisco, CA 94118
415-292-6260
tribal_art_dolls@hotmail.com

Joy Roberts-Hill
Doll-e-Mark
20-10L West Mosholu Pkwy. S.
Bronx, NY 10468
dollemark@yahoo.com

Mark Ruffin
PO Box 42139
Philadelphia, PA 19101
markeruffin@hotmail.com

Lorna Miller Sands
4969 Bender Ferry Rd.
Mount Juliet, TN 37122
615-758-3863
LornaM123@aol.com
www.geocities.com/
lornamillersands

Rotraut Schrott
Spitzingstrasse 1
85598 Baldham
Germany
011-49-8106-8031
fax: 011-49-8106-8680

LuLu Tatum
3239 Santa Barbara Blvd.
Cape Coral, FL33993
239-772-3585
520-205-0378

Gloria Tepper
10 Plaza St.
Brooklyn, NY 11238
718-399-2330
nn.tepper@verizon.net

Robert Tonner
Tonner Doll Company
459 Hurley Ave.
Hurley, NY 12443
845-339-9537
www.tonnerdoll.com

Sharon Tucker
6644 Lincoln Dr.
Philadelphia, PA 19119
215-629-2911
215-849-3339
sharontucker3@hotmail.com

Bets & Amy van Boxel
't Vaartje 14
5165 NB Waspik
The Netherlands
011-0-416-312134, phone
011-0-416-313571, fax
bets@poppenstee.nl
www.poppenstee.nl

Marcella Welch
Something for the Soul
5475 Route 193
Andover, OH 44003
440-293-7380
info@somethingforthesoul.com
www.somethingforthesoul.com

Paula Whaley
Oneeki Designs
2103 N. Charles St., Apt. H
Baltimore, MD 21218
202-588-7468
oneeki@aol.com

Goldie Wilson
Original Dolls by Goldie
8505 Edgeworth Dr.
Capitol Heights, MD 20743
301-350-4119
goldiewil@msn.com